Reminisc_____ ___
Observations of a
Hong Kong Chai Lo

Reminiscences and Observations of a Hong Kong Chai Lo

John Griffiths

The Pentland Press Limited
Edinburgh • Cambridge • Durham • USA

First published in 1997 by
The Pentland Press Ltd.
1 Hutton Close
South Church
Bishop Auckland
Durham

British Library Cataloguing in Publication Data.
A Catalogue record for this book is available
from the British Library.

ISBN 1 85821 470 X

Typeset by CBS, Felixstowe, Suffolk
Printed and bound by Antony Rowe Ltd., Chippenham

This book is dedicated to Claudia who provided the initial incentive to put the stories into print, to Roger who provided the encouragement to pursue the objective, to Pim for her patience and endless cups of coffee as I played with the computer and most importantly to colleagues in 'Asia's Finest'.

ACKNOWLEDGEMENTS

As all police officers know full well recollections of events are influenced by the perspective of the witness at the time of the event and time further distorts memories. There will be some colleagues who may think that they can recognize themselves in the following pages and a select few might well be correct but in most instances characters are composites as are some of the stories if only to protect the innocent and allow me some dramatic licence.

CONTENTS

PROLOGUE

He had indulged himself on this, his last flight out of Hong Kong and had treated himself to the luxury of a Business Class seat. As he boarded the aircraft, a solicitous member of the cabin staff showed him to his seat and assisted in stowing his hand baggage in the overhead locker then enquired if he would care for a drink whilst waiting for take-off. He stretched out in the seat and started to play with the buttons adjusting the seat to various positions of comfort, actions which would have immediately brought a reprimand back in Economy Class but now only produced a tolerant smile as he was handed his orange juice. He promptly decided that he had been unnecessarily depriving himself when he had travelled in Economy Class on previous flights and in future he would only travel Business Class.

He peered through the porthole beside him and gazed over the terminal building to the Kowloon Foothills which dominated the airport. Local legend was that the peninsular was named after the nine foothills (Kau Lung – nine hills) which guarded the area but he had never been able to find seven distinct peaks among the hills. Perhaps the skyline had changed even before his arrival; it certainly had changed since he first arrived. As the urban area of Kowloon had extended to the eastward so had the lower foothills disappeared. Much of the soil had been used to fill in the harbour which was significantly narrower now and he still felt that it was contrary to natural science for the sea current through the harbour to be slower than it was before the reclamation work started.

1

At last the aircraft started to taxi away from the terminal building and lumber ponderously towards the runway for take-off. In the air a Boeing 747 had a degree of majesty but on the ground it was like a beached whale. Slowly the aircraft gathered momentum and clawed its way up into the sky over Mount Davis and the concrete jungle that was Hong Kong faded into the haze. There was a last glimpse of the south side of Hong Kong Island with scores of junks bobbing in the glistening sea, then the aircraft turned away on its course over South China and the beckoning night. As he was served another glass of orange juice he asked to be alerted when the aircraft flew over the Himalayan Mountains; he never ceased to be fascinated by the vast snowbound landscape. He settled back in his seat and pondered his future.

The future was somewhat vague and a prospect to which he had given very little thought. Retirement was only for old men and he did not feel old, in fact in his last annual report he had been called a teenage geriatric. He had difficulty in reconciling the fact that he had served for over thirty-three years in the Royal Hong Kong Police Force and at the tender age of 54 he was now retiring, a pensioner, a member of the 'Over the Hill Mob'. He consoled himself with the fact the retirement had come a year earlier than anticipated as he, and other members of the Special Branch, were compulsorily retired to facilitate constitutional change in Hong Kong consequent upon the Agreement between the government of the United Kingdom and the government of the People's Republic of China under which the Crown Colony of Hong Kong reverts to Chinese Sovereignty in 1997. Typical Special Branch verbiage to explain the offer of a year's salary if he would leave Hong Kong as soon as possible.

He had remained in Hong Kong for his pre-retirement leave and had used the time to visit the Philippines and Thailand and indulge in the sun drenched, decadent luxury offered in those countries but now faced the prospect of living in the

2

bleaker climes of Wales.

He had been born and raised in Pembrokeshire which is sometimes referred to as 'Little England beyond Wales' and until he joined the Royal Navy the furthest he had been from home had been a weekend in London courtesy of the Air Training Corps. Initially, he had served as a Naval Air Cadet which was the lowest form of life recognized by the Admiralty. However, the equestrian skills he had acquired as a child found favour with the gunnery lieutenant whilst his cricketing skills found favour with the chief instructor so life was not too arduous.

His equestrian activities and his love of John Wayne movies brought him the sobriquet 'Cowboy' from his fellow cadets and somehow this name haunted him for the rest of his life. On his posting to a training squadron he found himself a midshipman, a rank that he had previously only associated with Hornblower. Here his prowess on the rugby field served to keep him out of serious trouble but did not help him to achieve his 'Wings' and after a few disastrous navigational errors their Lords Commissioners of the Admiralty felt it would be in the best interests of all if there was a parting of the ways.

Returning to Pembrokeshire was something of a cultural shock and he felt more than somewhat unsettled. It was fate that the day after seeing the film, *The World of Suzie Wong*, starring Nancy Kwan, he saw an advert for the Hong Kong Police Force in a national newspaper. In a rush of madness he sent off an application and two weeks later attended an Interview Board in London. The medical examination was quite superficial whilst the Interview Board seemed only interested in his reaction to serving under the command of Chinese officers. With little forethought or consideration on his behalf he found himself bound for Hong Kong.

From the beginning he had settled down in Hong Kong where he felt a comfortable affinity both with the people and with the environment. The seventies had been the most satisfying in that he had commanded the Special Branch VIP Protection Section which gave him a chance to play a John Wayne role in real life and he met and married a local Chinese solicitor with whom he shared his interest in horses and they operated a small equestrian school as a hobby. It was not surprising that the sobriquet 'Cowboy' was perpetuated during this period but at least now it was abbreviated to just that with the 'Wanchai' dropped. After over thirty years, it was coming to an end and the ageing 'Cowboy', now a widower, was flying off into his last sunset.

Hong Kong had changed over the last thirty years and in some ways he was glad to be leaving as the rate of change accelerated with the approach of 1997. He settled back in his seat and at first tried to watch a film on the tiny screen set in the back of the seat in front of him but could not focus on it clearly so he tried to read a book but that was equally unattractive. He lay back in the seat with a cigarette in hand and his mind wandered back in time to when the Cowboy first came to Hong Kong.

Chapter One

FIRST IMPRESSIONS

The British Overseas Airways Corporation flight from London with stopovers at Paris, Rome, Cairo, Bombay and Bangkok had taken almost twenty-five hours to reach Hong Kong by which time the Cowboy was in a state of complete mental numbness.

During the flight he had managed to strike up an acquaintanceship with the passenger seated beside him. Initially, the Cowboy was a little hesitant as this was the first Chinese with whom he had ever spoken and he was a little curious about the people among whom he was going to live for the next three years. Unbeknown to the Cowboy, Henry LIM was in fact very Westernised and anything but a typical Hong Kong Chinese. During their conversation the Cowboy gathered that LIM came from a fairly wealthy family and his father was the owner and headmaster of the Tak Ming Middle School, a large private school in Mong Kok. His sister, Mona, had been educated in the United States whilst his elder brother, Gus LIM, had been a pilot with the United States Air Force and was now a sub-inspector in the Hong Kong Police Force.

This last news had provided a form of common link in that the Cowboy was on his way to Hong Kong to join the police force. Henry LIM had recently graduated from Oxford University with his Masters Degree for which his thesis had been the history of Ting Kau, a small fishing village on the west coast of the New Territories. The Hong Kong that Henry LIM described, in his flawless English, was vastly different from that which the Cowboy had imagined but then his ideas

5

were based on films he had seen which was hardly a sound basis. As the aircraft prepared to land the Cowboy inquired if LIM could recommend a tailor as he would need some clothes suitable for the hot, humid climate of Hong Kong and felt a slight jar of discomfort when LIM casually commented that on the salary of a police sub-inspector the Cowboy would not be able to afford to use the same tailor.

On touching down the Cowboy experienced the Hong Kong arrival for the first time: almost everyone ignored the pleas of the stewardesses, as they were termed in the days before political correctness, and stood up scrambling to get their belongings together for arrival. The Cowboy remained seated, completely amazed at the chaos around him, and only stirred when a stewardess pointed out that the aircraft was almost empty. He walked slowly down the ramp to the tarmac and straggled after the other passengers towards a large Nissen shed which apparently housed the immigration services. He gazed around, taking in the hills surrounding the airport to the north and east, with Hong Kong Island rising from the sea to the south, and marvelled at the skill of the pilot who had managed such a smooth landing.

He entered the Nissen shed and just stood watching the crowd thronging around the immigration counters. A Chinese in a stiffly starched short-sleeved khaki shirt and knee length shorts approached him and asked if he was the expected police recruit from England. The Cowboy acknowledged that he was and identified himself and the Chinese, who identified himself as Sub-Inspector CHOW, apologized for not using the Cowboy's name but he had not known how to pronounce it. The Cowboy pointed out that many other Europeans had arrived on the same flight and inquired what had led CHOW straight to him. CHOW laughed and replied that the Cowboy was the only one who strolled along looking around whilst everyone else had been in a hurry. CHOW led the Cowboy off through the crowd to the Crew Channel explaining that the

Immigration Service was part of the Special Branch of the Police Force hence the landing formalities could be expedited in comfort.

After collecting his battered navy issue suitcase, the Cowboy was escorted to a large dark-blue lorry with the letters 'Police' painted on the side. CHOW spoke to the driver and then they departed, with the Cowboy sitting in solitary splendour in the back, for the Police Training School at Wong Chuk Hang. The journey through Kowloon was a blur of people and noise to which the interlude on the Cross Harbour Vehicular Ferry was a pleasant break. The harbour teemed with vessels of all sizes and styles ranging from little sampans, sculled by females dressed in black outfits topped with large flat straw hats, to stately junks tacking before the cross breezes within the harbour, powerful motor boats, dirty rust-patched freighters and imposing ocean-going liners.

On reaching the Island the lorry followed a twisting road up around Victoria Peak then down towards the fishing village of Aberdeen. The Cowboy was amazed at the panorama unfolding before him but was careful not to look down too closely at the sheer drop beside the road. On arrival at the Police Training School the Cowboy noticed that the driver's uniform was dark with sweat and realised that it had been a considerate gesture on the parts of CHOW and the driver to seat him in the back where the breeze had provided some respite from the heat.

The Police Training School was a former army camp originally built by the Japanese during their occupation of Hong Kong and converted during the fifties into a training school. The quarters for the recruit sub-inspectors was a converted Rice Godown partitioned off to provide sleeping accommodation and a general Mess area. The training staff had already left for the day when the Cowboy arrived and the duty student showed him to his bed space then left. He barely had time to dump his belongings before some fellow recruits came in and introductions were made. On confirming that he had money left over from the advance paid by the Crown Agents they invited him to join them on a visit to Wanchai. As it was Saturday and the following day being a rest day, there was no curfew that night. He borrowed a towel and after a quick shave and shower he joined six other recruits crushed into a Volkswagen driven by Peter Ozoeuf and off they went to Wanchai.

The Cowboy was not sure just what he expected but he had harboured a romantic yearning for Chinese girls after developing a teenage crush on Judy Dan, and covering the underside of his school desk top with photographs of her until caught by the headmaster and made to remove them. He was not disappointed when he entered the first bar and, much to the cynical amusement of his three-month seasoned new colleagues, he just sat and watched as exotic Chinese girls in figure hugging cheung shaams (long gowns with hip-high slits) jiggled around him.

They visited several bars in the course of the evening and the Cowboy had his first plate of Yuk Sze Chow Mein (fried noodles with pork) at a Taai Pai Dong (cooked food stall) on the pavement in Luard Road. It was close to midnight when the group made it to the 83 Bar which was the police officers' current favourite watering-hole in Wanchai. There he met Evan Evans whom he knew from his school days when they had competed against each other, Evans having attended the local rival school. The first time the Cowboy had represented his school at cricket he had been clean bowled first ball by Evans, an ignominy that was burnt into his schoolhood memories.

After a somewhat boisterous reunion Evans, who had been in Hong Kong over two years, took him under his wing to protect him from freeloaders and predators and introduced him to a petite young Chinese girl dressed in a tight black cheung shaam which did little to disguise her exquisite figure. Her thick black hair flowed down on either side of a centre

8

parting to flirt with her shoulders. Although only 20 years old, Jenny was a seasoned Wanchai Warrior and the Cowboy fell in lust with her as soon as she sat beside him in the bar booth and rested her tiny hand on his thigh. At the suggestion of Evans they adjourned to the cockloft above the bar where the besotted Cowboy bought her several 'ladies drinks' – small glasses of Chinese tea at $2.40 per drink – and stared with unconcealed interest at the glimpses of white thigh and firm buttocks that were on display. However, he was far too inhibited to do anything but stare. At closing time Evans came to the rescue and, after conversing with Jenny in Cantonese, turned to the Cowboy and told him that he was in luck as Jenny was going to take him home for the night to celebrate, 12th July 1960, his first night in Hong Kong.

The pair left the bar together and Jenny tottered along on her three-inch stiletto heels, her arm firmly in the crook of his and her head well below his shoulder. Looking down at her, the Cowboy was filled with a sense of protective fulfilment induced by this exotic but fragile creature beside him. They walked around the block and down Jaffe Road, lined with old colonial-style three storey buildings with green shutters to most first floor windows, until they reached an old tenement building. A top-floor cubicle was home for Jenny.

The Cowboy suddenly developed an attack of shyness coupled with embarrassment much to the obvious amusement of the young girl. Giggling happily to herself, Jenny introduced him to the intricacies of removing a cheung shaam, starting with a pair of hooks at the collar, a row of press studs from the neck to the armpit and a zipper from there to the waist. When she stepped out of the cheung shaam and stood before him dressed only in a small black bra and black panties the Cowboy thought that he was in heaven; nothing like this ever happened in the valleys of Wales. Jenny helped him out of his shirt and trousers which she carefully placed on a coat-hanger and which she hung behind the door. Then she took his hand

9

and led him to the bed. The rest of the night passed in a dream that was to remain etched indelibly in his memory for the next thirty years. It was everything that Richard Mason had described in his book and far, far more.

In the morning Jenny produced some Chinese tea and afterwards took him down to the street where she hailed a taxi and gave the driver instructions on where to take the Cowboy. He was thankful for this as he had no idea where the Police Training School was much less how to get there.

On the following Wednesday several of the recruits were taken to the Police Sports Club on Boundary Street in Kowloon where training had already started for the next rugby season. On the return journey the Cowboy could no longer resist the urge to visit Wanchai and there was no problem in persuading the driver to drop him off in the vicinity. The Cowboy went directly to the 83 Bar to find Jenny. He sat at a booth near the counter and shortly afterwards Jenny slid into the bench seat beside him. They sat together talking. Jenny had a fairly good command of fractured English spiced with American idioms, though he winced once or twice at some of the coarser phrases that she used in all innocence. To the Cowboy there was a curious mixture of girl and woman about Jenny that he found intriguing. He was in love and it came as a blow to his ego to find that as far as Jenny was now concerned he was just another customer, her customer, but not her boy friend. He was no longer a Wanchai Cherry Boy (virgin) and there were no special favours.

During that week two more expatriate probationary sub-inspectors arrived from the United Kingdom. John Morgan, a blond blue-eyed youth, who, strangely, came from the Valleys of Wales and had served as a second lieutenant in the Paratroop Regiment during his National Service. The other was Jack Fidler who was in his late twenties and had served as a detective constable with the Lancashire Police Force before a disagreement with his detective sergeant had induced him

10

to resign and join the Hong Kong Force. To the new recruits, Fidler was an old hand and they tended to look to him for leadership and guidance.

The following Monday morning the trio were instructed to dress smartly and report to Police Headquarters by 10 am for an interview with Mr Bidemead, the Deputy Commissioner of Police. They were in the waiting room on the fifth floor of Police Headquarters by 9.45 am only to discover that the interview had in fact been scheduled for eleven and they had to cool their heels waiting. On the dot of eleven they were ushered into the presence of the Deputy Commissioner who came around his desk to shake their hands and welcome them to the Force. He inquired about their backgrounds and nodded approvingly on hearing that the Cowboy had been commissioned in the Royal Navy and that Morgan had been commissioned in the Army. On hearing that Fidler had only held the rank of lance-corporal in an infantry regiment during his National Service he grunted his disapproval and thereafter ignored Fidler. He told the Cowboy and Morgan that there was a satisfying career ahead for recruits from their background and warned them to keep out of the honky-tonks of Wanchai and be sure that they ate their peas off the back of their forks. Bidemead warned them about forming any relationship with native Chinese girls though, as healthy young men, they might be expected to sow some wild oats with discretion.

On the way back to the training school the trio were still in a state of bewilderment at the interview and on arrival they immediately approached John 'Sailor' England, their course instructor, to tell him about it. England explained that Bidemead was from the old colonial school of officer who were, thankfully, a dying breed. He informed them that up to only two years previously if a police officer married a local Chinese girl the marriage was not recognized by the Force and the officer was denied all marriage privileges. Further, entering into a marriage with a local Chinese girl was a bar to any future promotion within the Force. The only exception being if the girl came from a local Portuguese or Macanese family. England added that there was some justification for this attitude in that the different cultural and educational backgrounds created considerable strain on any relationship and, often, the families did not approve which did not help. As a result many mixed marriages broke down within a couple of years.

Generally, the Chinese did not socialize with foreigners and a Chinese girl from a respectable family was most unlikely to have anything to do with a foreigner. If she did, she and her family would lose face as the only Chinese girls who would normally socialize with foreigners in public were bar girls. In other words prostitutes, who were not really suitable marriage partners for expatriate police officers because of their backgrounds, their lack of education and the cultural differences.

Each night at the training school one recruit sub-inspector did a tour in the duty room with one of the instructors. There was little hardship in this duty and most evenings were spent sitting on the verandah outside the duty room sipping cold beers. Lined up on the verandah, mounted on tripods were three large telescopes which were focused on the nurses' quarters of the Grantham Hospital across the valley. Much of the evening's entertainment was gained from watching the quarters especially when there was a change of shift. It reminded the Cowboy of the game of 'mine sweepers' he had played as a child when the officers called out sightings to each other, 'second floor, fourth window', etc. Some of the nurses seemed to have no inhibitions about changing without lowering the blinds and some were so exhibitionist that the officers sometimes wondered if the nurses were aware of the watchers.

One night the Cowboy was on duty with Gus LIM and

12

since the mist over the alley precluded their normal entertainment they just talked. The conversation took a more serious tone when LIM discussed corruption in Hong Kong and warned the Cowboy that when he left the training school he would soon come across it. LIM compared corruption to a raging river and advised the Cowboy that he could either stand on the bank and watch it flow past or jump in and flow with the current. Any attempt to swim up stream would only end in disaster.

He explained that in China corruption was a traditional way of life and, although there had been over 100 years of colonial rule, it still existed in Hong Kong. For example, in a restaurant one paid a tip in order to gain special service or extra attention from a waiter and in the real world one paid 'tea money' to a government official to obtain special attention. Much of the corruption in the police force was related to, what LIM termed, 'social crime' where there were no innocent victims. A drug addict was not forced to take drugs, a gambler was not forced to gamble whilst girls were not forced to become prostitutes other than by their own economic circumstances. Police influence in these spheres prevented any abuses in the form of blackmail, enforcers etc. This influence also provided a valuable source of information in that gambling, sex and drugs were the main motives for 'real' crime and the police did not tolerate 'real' crime in which there were always innocent victims. The Cowboy was still a naive country boy from rural Wales and found it difficult to accept the rationale put forward by LIM but at the same time conceded there was some form of logic to it.

During familiarization tours in the early months at the Police Training School the Cowboy discovered that although the Colony of Hong Kong occupied only a relatively small area there were definite physical and social divisions. Hong Kong Island, normally referred to simply as the Island, was separated from the Mainland by the waters of the Harbour and an attitude of social superiority held by its inhabitants. Passage across the waters was provided by the Star Ferry and the Jordan Road Vehicular Ferry both of which closed down overnight.

All the major financial and commercial concerns established their offices in Central District on the Island though a few recognized the existence of Kowloon by establishing small branch offices over there. A commercial enterprise that did not have an address in Central was viewed with a degree of suspicion as regards its financial soundness. This attitude led to some small concerns renting desk space in a Central office to provide a respectable address for their letterheads whilst the actual business was conducted elsewhere.

On the Island it was considered necessary for expatriates to reside on the Peak, or at least at Mid Levels; anywhere else was not socially acceptable. Those unfortunates who did live elsewhere were viewed as being a little eccentric or to have gone native. Police officers who were generally required to reside in the stations in which they served were looked upon with pity and were definitely below the salt in the social pecking order. Crossing the Harbour was considered an excursion to the extent that, in later years, the Cowboy once heard a senior officer proudly declaim that in over twenty-five years service the only times he had been to Kowloon were when arriving or departing via the airport.

Kowloon was a sprawling mass spreading out on either side from Nathan Road which was in those days a sleepy boulevard lined with banyan trees. Tsim Sha Tsui, at the tip of the peninsula, was acceptable if only because it was the location of the premier hotel in Hong Kong, the historic and pretentious Peninsula Hotel. North of Austin Road was not acceptable and, in fact in the sixties, most of Yaumatei and Mong Kok Districts were out of bounds to members of the British Forces, being considered the Chinese Quarter. Whilst the foothills to the north from which the area derives its name

14

Kowloon (Kau Lung – Nine Hills) were festooned with flimsy structures that housed refugees from China in appalling conditions.

The New Territories which were leased from China in 1899 lurked on the other side of the foothills and after a couple of conducted tours the Cowboy came to the conclusion that little had changed since 1899. The killing of an alleged man-eating tiger in Sheung Shui around 1926 was still a serious topic of conversation. The Japanese had advanced through the New Territories in December 1941 they had never succeeded in securing the area, which for most of the Occupation period remained under the sway of the Communist East River Guerrilla Column. The remaining division of the Colony was the Outlying Islands where small fishing communities continued their traditional way of life.

Most Saturday nights the Cowboy visited Wanchai and slowly discovered that there was an unwritten code of conduct among the bar girls. An overseas visitor was fair game for any girl and commercial sex could be available on an ascending scale depending on the nationality of the customer. A European was the cheapest rate, followed by an Australian; an American was more expensive. Generally, an expatriate businessman in Hong Kong could negotiate a special rate using the Mama-san as intermediary.

However, money was not the sole criterion and the girls retained a large degree of choice in the matter and would, at times, refuse a customer on the grounds of his uncouthness, attitude or even dirty finger nails. In the case of servicemen some bar girls would only go out with officers whilst a few even differentiated between Americans from the northern states and the southern states and would only give their favours to the latter as they were gentlemen and treated them with respect.

As always, there were the few who would go out with anyone who had the money to pay for them. These girls were held in contempt by the others as having no class or style. Negotiations required great diplomatic skills on the part of the Mama-san to avoid offending the customer and possibly pointing him towards another girl who was less particular.

In those days the majority of the Mama-sans originated from Shanghai as did many of the bar girls who were generally taller and better built than their compatriots from southern China. There was a marked cultural distinction between the Shanghaiese and the Cantonese which, surprisingly, was more often the cause of dispute than anything else. The Shanghaiese girls were very skilled at assessing the potential of any customer and within a few minutes of a customer entering a bar would have a shrewd idea of how much he intended to spend. The bar girls themselves would seldom openly hustle for 'ladies drinks' but would leave this to the Mama-san to suggest, or else induce the customer to invite them to join him in a drink – a particularly opportune moment being when the customer ordered his own drink.

The expatriate police officers who frequented the bars were generally treated as casual friends and not as potential customers as the girls knew full well that the officers earned less than many of them in a good month, hence they were not commercially attractive clients. During quiet periods when they were not playing cards some of the girls would chat with the officers with the result that a number of officers spoke Cantonese with a distinct Shanghai accent and unconsciously used female rather than male phrases and terminology. The younger police officers tended to go to the bars to socialize among themselves in a more relaxed surrounding than the police Messes which were inhabited by senior officers.

Many bars offered special low prices (Pong-Pan Prices) to police officers to attract their regular custom and one night the Cowboy asked BUTT Choi-sum, the manager/owner of the Savoy Bar, the reason for this privilege.

BUTT replied that although he only made a few cents on

16

each drink the volume of business over a month covered most of his routine overheads, but more importantly the presence of the police officers attracted business. A tourist would bypass a quiet, empty bar but would feel comfortable going into a bar where there was a group of cheerful customers.

The bar girls projected a brassy, commercial image and, in some instances, particularly among the older girls seasoned with bitter experience, this was a true reflection of their attitude. In many instances, however, it was a false image and under the facade they were very vulnerable and insecure young girls.

The expatriate police officer was expected to pay court to a girl for several weeks and become her regular 'boy friend' before he enjoyed her favours. Thereafter he was her man and the focus of jealous tantrums if he so much as looked at another girl, even if it were in another bar. There was a very effective grapevine between the bars. Any customer who bought a girl out and took her to bed then, the next time, moved on to another girl was considered bad news and was termed a 'Taai Wooi Ying' (butterfly). A simple conversation with another girl was viewed with grave suspicion and barely tolerated, whilst to buy a drink for another girl was a serious betrayal and any breaches of this unwritten code of etiquette on the part of a police officer was an unforgivable sin. One officer carried the sobriquet of 'Taai Wooi Ying' as a result of a single indiscretion until he retired some thirty years later. Any attempt to present a rational defence by pointing out that the girl had entertained other customers was ignored; she was just doing business but his conduct amounted to a loss of face for her.

Gentleman Jim Howard was in his second tour in Hong Kong and enjoyed a long established relationship with Grace from the Ocean Bar in Lockhart Road. As implied by his nickname, Jim took great pride in his appearance and was always elegantly attired in the latest fashions. His extensive

17

wardrobe of suits and tailored shirts represented his total income over the years and not a few of the items were presents from Grace who was very proud of her man. One night Jim was out with friends in Kowloon and met a young girl in one of the Carnarvon Road bars. Feeling reasonably safe, being on the other side of the Harbour, he took the girl out to dinner and enjoyed her company until dawn when he arose and took a Walla Walla (small motor boat) back to Hong Kong Island.

Unfortunately for Jim, the local grapevine was in fine form that night and Grace was well aware of his escapade long before he returned home. When he got home, he took a shower then went to his wardrobe to take out fresh clothes and discovered to his horror that the sleeves had been cut off all his jackets and shirts whilst all his trousers were now shorts. He did not have to be told who was the culprit nor the reason for her actions.

The Hong Kong bars enjoyed an intelligence service that would have been the envy of any intelligence corps, particularly in respect of the movements of ships of the United States Navy. It was not unusual for signs to go up around the bars welcoming specific ships days before the vessels entered Hong Kong waters and, during the Vietnam conflict, the leakage of this information caused concern to the occupants of the US Consulate on Garden Road. As soon as the girls knew which ship was due to arrive they would check their notebooks to see which boy friends were coming and ensure that their correspondence was up to date.

The majority of the girls could only speak limited English. They were less able to read and write it and this is where the police officers came to the rescue. A friendly police officer would read and translate the incoming mail and in return for a beer would compose a suitable reply. Naturally, some officers were better than others at composing replies and it developed into a competition between them as to who could compose the most romantic reply. When some replies produced concrete results in the form of US dollars the competition took a different aspect and the standard of composition was judged on the results it produced. Mothers falling downstairs and needing hospitalization or younger brothers in need of school fees were common themes, whilst a natural disaster or a typhoon was a blessing for those needing inspiration. After a couple of incidents arising from similar letters being received by shipmates on the same vessel, copies of letters were retained and a simple cross referencing system set up to avoid repetitions.

One evening the Cowboy was sitting alone in the Savoy Bar in Carnarvon Road when an American customer was enjoying the attentions of several bar girls including San San who was the Cowboy's current girl friend, which probably accounted for the morose expression on the Cowboy's face. After about an hour the American called for his bill and promptly expressed his outrage at the size of it.

The Mama-san approached the table and the American complained loudly that he had been cheated and that his bill was padded. The Mama-san took the offending bill amounting to several hundred dollars and just tore it in half, then asked the man quietly to leave as it was an honest bar and did not need cheapskate customers like him. The Cowboy could not believe his ears and after the American had left he asked the Mama-san what she thought she was doing. She just smiled and, putting the torn bill in a safe place, told the Cowboy to wait for an hour then the American would be back.

It was just under an hour later when the American, a little sheepishly, entered the bar again and apologized to the Mama-san for his outburst. He settled his bill then sat down to spend even more money during the course of that evening and returned each evening for the next three nights. When the Cowboy asked the Mama-san to explain how she knew that the American would return she pointed to the expensive well-cut attire, polite cultured voice, full wallet and the fact that he was staying at the Peninsula Hotel. These, to her, were the signs of a wealthy gentleman and her experience told her that he would realize his mistake and when he did so he would spend even more money to assuage his sense of guilt.

Not all customers were treated in such fashion and on other occasions the Mama-san would turn into a fiercesome harridan and obtain immediate and full settlement of all accounts.

Chapter Two

ON THE BEAT

On 4th February 1961, some seven months after his arrival in Hong Kong, the Cowboy graduated from the Police Training School and, together with Morgan and Fidler, was posted to Yaumatei Division in Kowloon Police District. The following Monday the trio were formally interviewed by Divisional Superintendent, WONG Wing-ying, who was known to all as 'Mambo'. The interview followed the usual lines but the Cowboy found it somewhat odd to listen to this very Chinese-looking officer talking in accentless English about his home in Scotland. It was clear, however, that 'Mambo' was the equivalent to God as far as new recruits were concerned and it did not seem inappropriate when he directed that if they had any problems they should seek the advice of the Uniform Branch Staff Sergeant who he equated to the company sergeant major in the army and was normally referred to as 'Major'.

The Cowboy soon discovered that policing in Hong Kong was vastly different from any preconceptions he had formed and which were based on the traditional village bobby and Jack Warner in *Dixon of Dock Green*. Kowloon Police District was divided into four police divisions each commanded by a superintendent and each division divided into two sub-divisions each commanded by a long serving sub-inspector. In time of emergency each division was expected to field a riot company of 120 personnel and riot drill was held twice a month. Around the station building strategic posts for 'Attack on Station' were numbered in red and drills were practised at frequent intervals.

Key senior inspectorate officers were required to live in married quarters within the station compound and most expatriate inspectorate officers lived in Messes in the station building. There were blocks of married quarters for expatriate inspectorate and a few blocks of married quarters for long serving junior officers but most of the single junior officers lived in dormitories in the compound. There were virtually no married quarters for married local inspectorate officers and no quarters provided for single local inspectorate though if there were vacant rooms some lived in the expatriate Messes. This facilitated the provision of an instant reserve in time of emergency and half of the next shift to go on duty were required to be in the station on station reserve at all times.

The NCOs and constables in Uniform Branch were always referred to by the numbers on their shoulder badges whilst there was some relaxation within the CID and some were referred to by name or nickname though always by their number on formal occasions.

Each sub-division was divided into a number of beats with a few static points such as street markets or key points. Constables were expected to march briskly along their designated beats and reach specified check points every fifteen minutes. Any constable who stopped to talk with a member of the public was required to record the purpose of the conversation in his official notebook and failure to so do was a disciplinary offence of 'Gossiping on Duty'. The police force was very much a paramilitary formation organized on very military lines and an environment in which most of the expatriates felt at ease since most had completed their National Service in the United Kingdom. However, it was also an environment that emphasized the separation of the Force from the Public and to some of the officers it gave the feeling of being an occupation force rather than a police force serving the public.

For the first two weeks the new trio carried out their patrols in the company of a slightly more experienced sub-inspector and thereafter they were left to their own devices. The Cowboy was very conscious of the language and cultural barriers that existed between himself and the constables he was supposed to be supervising and between himself and members of the public. He studied hard at his Cantonese and practised phrases that could be used in his contacts with the constables and the public.

One day he came across some hawkers who were obstructing the pavement which gave him an opportunity to ask them politely in Cantonese to move on as they were causing an obstruction. The hawkers looked at him in amazement and some could scarcely conceal their mirth which somewhat disconcerted the Cowboy who tried his practised phrases again but to no avail. A constable then came to his rescue and advised him that the appropriate phrase was 'Hang Gau Hui' and this had the desired effect. Later he asked his language tutor the meaning of the phrase and was even more disconcerted to learn that it meant 'Fuck off'. So much for being polite and earning the respect of the public.

A few months later the police district held a formal Ball in one of the larger hotels in Tsim Sha Tsui which required the expenditure of more than one month's salary for purchase of a dinner jacket plus the cost of the tickets. None of the young inspectors knew of any suitable partners for such a formal social function and all decided to volunteer for duty that night in order to avoid the expenditure. The lack of response from his young officers came to the attention of WONG who called all into his office and directed that they would attend.

On the day, the officers assembled in a bar in Tsim Sha Tsui to have a few cheap drinks first and as an expression of their resentment were deliberately some fifteen minutes late arriving at the ballroom.

Entering the room they discovered that they had been

allocated a front table by the dance floor and as they made their way across the room WONG could be seen sitting alone at the head of the table with an expression on his face that clearly indicated his concealed rage at their discourtesy. He gestured for them to sit along one side of the table and the Cowboy who had been slow off the mark found himself seated on the right of WONG.

The officers had barely taken their seats when a group of very attractive young Chinese ladies made their way to the table and sat in the seats opposite the officers. Mambo had arranged for ten starlets from Shaw Brothers' Film Studio to join his table for the evening. The reaction of the officers seemed to satisfy WONG who swiftly relaxed and took up the role of the genial host. A most enjoyable evening followed and the presence of the bevy of beauties at their table made the officers the envy of officers from other divisions but the end of the Ball proved to be somewhat of an anti-climax when the ladies left as a group to return to their quarters at the film studio.

It was not long after the Ball that the Cowboy decided to sit for his First Colloquial Cantonese Certificate, the examination for which was conducted by a board of three chaired by the District Police Commander. The Cowboy was lucky and achieved a pass with distinction which meant that he would receive a bonus of one month's salary. However, the District Police Commander commented that whilst the Cowboy had a good vocabulary he needed to work on his fluency and suggested a sleeping dictionary would be useful.

The next day the Cowboy went out and spent most of the bonus on the purchase of a record player and long playing language records which he dutifully played each night as he went to sleep. After some weeks of doing this one of his colleagues asked him why he played these dull records every night and the Cowboy explained. There was complete silence in the Mess for at least a minute before everyone burst into laughter and it was several minutes before anyone had recovered sufficiently to explain to the Cowboy that a sleeping dictionary meant a Chinese girl friend. Years later this anecdote about the Cowboy's naivete still surfaced to his embarrassment.

Whilst on patrol the Cowboy found his way around all the side streets and back alleys of Yaumatei and Mong Kok which were the two sub-divisions of Yaumatei Division. On Nathan Road, which ran through the middle of both sub-divisions, his presence generally attracted little attention but away from the main thoroughfare it was not unusual for him to pick up a 'tail' of young children who walked behind him, watching the antics of the strange Gwai Lo (foreign devil) with large round eyes. Attempts to converse with them were never successful as they merely scattered and then slowly regrouped and followed again until he left their area. On report room duty it was not uncommon for a parent, usually the mother, to drag her errant offspring into the station for a scolding by the police officer for not doing their homework or some other misdeed.

One night the Cowboy was on duty in the report room when an aged crone came into the station in great distress. Slowly it emerged that someone had stolen her life savings of several thousand dollars which she had kept hidden under her pillow on her bed space. The Cowboy realized that CID would not appreciate it since it would be virtually impossible to detect the crime and CID existed on the crime detection returns – a detection rate falling below seventy-five per cent was the subject of consternation and if it continued for a second month the subject of wholesale transfers and inefficiency reports. However, he felt sorry for the old crone and passed the report to CID for enquiries, cynically wondering just how they would manage to write it off as a loss or accident. An hour or so later the old crone came out of the CID office clutching a bundle of money and thanking LUI Lok, the CID 'Major', for finding her money which she had so carelessly lost. As he crossed the report room LUI muttered something to the Cowboy which a constable later translated as LUI not being able to afford any more cases that night.

A few weeks later the Cowboy was again on the night-shift. Patrolling along Shanghai Street on his way back to the station, he met Constable 1234 at his scheduled check-point. The two officers continued on their way and just as the Cowboy was entering the station he heard some muffled bangs in the distance which he could not identify. Clarification came within a minute when it was reported that Constable 1234 had been shot outside the Kwong Wah Hospital in Dundas Street.

The Duty Officer sounded the 'Attack on Station' siren to summon the station reserve whilst the Cowboy sped back to the scene which was only a few hundred yards away. On arrival he found the constable had already been placed inside an ambulance and attending doctors from the adjacent hospital were adjusting drips. He gathered that the young constable had espied a burglar climbing out of a building and had given chase which had led out of Shanghai Street and down Nathan Road when two other constables appeared coming up Nathan Road. The burglar had turned into Dundas Street and ducked into an alley way. As the constable followed him into the alley way the burglar had hit him over the head then pulled the constable's gun out and shot him three times in the stomach before making good his escape.

The Cowboy started along the alley way and at the other end near Tung Choi Street he found a newspaper vendor who indicated that the culprit had run into Yin Chong Street. There the Cowboy found a car cleaner but he was not at all forthcoming and for a moment the Cowboy thought he might be the culprit. Less than fifteen minutes had elapsed since the shooting and there were already over 100 officers including some from adjacent stations cordoning off the area. With some amusement the Cowboy saw one expatriate officer dressed in rubber thongs and underpants with a riot helmet on his head and a Sterling sub-machine-gun under his arm. The Sub-Divisional Inspector and some CID officers joined the Cowboy in questioning the car cleaner but equally to no avail. Into the midst of this chaos came LUI Lok, dressed immaculately in blazer and slacks and every Brilliantined hair in place.

LUI took the car cleaner to one side and they hunched conspiratorially as LUI dug into his pocket and drew out a wad of several hundred dollars which changed hands. LUI then returned and calmly pointed to an old apartment building down the street and suggested that someone should try a cubicle on the third floor. Moments later officers did as suggested and found the burglar still dressed in his blood-spattered clothes.

Needless to say, the culprit was taken back to the station where he was later charged with attempted murder. Later the charge was reduced to wounding with intent and he pleaded guilty and was sentenced. A few weeks later the Cowboy was in the Administration Office when the dispatches arrived and he saw a memo from CID Headquarters which stated that since it was a straightforward wounding case which had been resolved very expeditiously, LUI Lok was only entitled to claim $50 in information money for the case.

One day WONG summoned the Cowboy to his office for a routine interview as it was approaching the first anniversary of the Cowboy's arrival in Hong Kong and more importantly the time for the Cowboy's annual incremental report. Apparently, WONG was pleased with the reports on the progress made by the Cowboy though he was not receptive to the Cowboy's criticism of the patrol system. During the interview WONG commented that he was becoming disturbed by the increasing number of under age girls working in the local low-class dance halls and directed that in future the Cowboy should pay particular attention to this problem when carrying out licence checks. In future, reports concerning under age girls were to be copied to him and he would arrange to interview them himself. Not only was this a personal directive from 'God' but a chance to impress.

The Cowboy carried out licence checks at every opportunity and usually managed to find two or three under age girls each week. One of the girls called Dan Mei was an attractive 15-year-old, a girl-woman, with a shy presence which was particularly appealing. The Cowboy thought nothing more about the incident for about a year then again he came across Dan Mei, this time in the Oriental Ballroom which was a most prestigious establishment of its type. He was a little taken aback at the hostility Dan Mei displayed towards him. This only served to intrigue him more. So when he was off duty he returned and invested in several 'dance hours' to secure her company.

Slowly Dan Mei relaxed and eventually she told him that he had 'jing kwu ngoh' (set her up) and the Cowboy hotly denied this.

Eventually, Dan Mei related that during her interview with WONG the latter had told her to stay home for a week and await a telephone call from him. A few days passed then WONG telephoned her and instructed that she dress in her old school clothes and meet him at a coffee shop in Prince Edwards Road. She did as instructed and over soft drinks in the coffee shop WONG had made it clear that she was to do as she was told and if she did so then she would be looked after. Dan Mei felt that she had no choice so she agreed. WONG then drove her to the Carlton Hotel on the Tai Po Road where he escorted her to a suite. A few minutes later a middle-aged European senior police officer came in and Dan Mei was introduced to him then WONG had left. During that afternoon the European indulged in his sexual fantasies with Dan Mei then sent her on her way with a few hundred dollars and this routine was repeated on a weekly basis for several months.

Shortly after her sixteenth birthday WONG had introduced her to a Mama-san at the Oriental Ballroom where she was now employed. Whilst she was appreciative of her rise to success in the sleazy world in which she was working, she still felt resentful about the manner in which it had come about and this resentment was focused upon the Cowboy.

The Cowboy was highly indignant over the way he had been used but he also recognized the officer from Dan Mei's description and realized that there was nothing he could do about it. The Oriental Ballroom was very expensive so the Cowboy could not afford to visit very often but whenever he did he would try to engage Dan Mei for a few dance hours as he felt a guilty responsibility for her. A year later the Cowboy was genuinely delighted to learn that Dan Mei had married a wealthy businessman and was now a respectable 'Tai Tai' (married woman of substance).

In December 1961 the Cowboy was summoned to the office of Mambo WONG, the Divisional Superintendent, and informed that he had passed all his Standard 2 Professional Examinations with Credit in his first attempt which was a commendable achievement and, that in the interests of his career advancement, he was to be posted to North Kowloon Magistracy as a court prosecutor. The Cowboy was quite cheerful at the news and promptly adjourned to the Mess to celebrate. The more cynical of his colleagues suggested that the transfer might be related to the fact that over each of the past four months he had brought more drug and gambling cases to court than the whole Vice Squad but at that time he did not really care since the transfer brought regular hours, no more shift duty and alternate week ends off.

Chapter Three

COURT STORIES

The Traffic Case

Jimmy MacDonald awoke with a groan and at the slightest movement of his head a gang of coolies armed each with a pneumatic drill started to prepare new canals through his skull.

It was, perhaps, not surprising since he had been ambushed by his Fokis (constables) at a Taai Sik Wooi (celebration dinner) the previous night and they had challenged him to Yam Shing (bottoms up) with them. In the course of less than an hour they had induced him to put away the best part of a bottle of XO brandy. He did not even like brandy but after the first glass caution had blown away like an umbrella in a typhoon and he only had vague recollections of the latter part of the night.

He was vaguely aware of water running in the bathroom and then to his surprise a young Chinese girl emerged from the bathroom draped in his bathrobe which was far too large for her and served to exaggerate her diminutive stature. On seeing him stir the girl giggled as Chinese girls tend to do when embarrassed, then crossed the room and sat on the bed beside him. Vague images of visiting the New Tonnachy Ballroom jogged his memory but refused to focus clearly in his mind.

'Jimee drink too much,' murmured the young girl, she giggled then added, 'Jimee take shower, feel better.'

Jimmy doubted if he would ever feel better and once more swore a solemn oath that he would never ever again drink brandy. The girl put a shower-cooled hand on his brow and gently stroked it. The movement was soothing and he was just getting used to it when the alarm clock on the bedside table shattered the growing tranquillity. He sat up with a start then wished that he had never moved and sank back on the bed.

Jimmy was in no fit state to go to court that morning and in any event the prospect of lying back and again surrendering to the tender administrations of the girl seemed far more appealing. Gesturing to the girl to keep quiet, he stretched across to the telephone and laboriously dialled the office number. When Philip Alcock, the officer-in-charge of the court staff, answered the telephone Jimmy croaked that he was feeling rough, probably due to something he had eaten, and was not up to coming to court that morning. Alcock, who by this time had already heard snatches about the previous night's revelry, sounded a little sarcastic when he replied that it was probably something that Jimmy had drunk rather than eaten. However, he accepted the flimsy excuse realizing full well that Jimmy would only be a liability as a prosecutor if he did come in. Jimmy relaxed and lay back, looked at the girl, then wondered just how he was going to find out her name without too much embarrassment to either party.

That morning the Cowboy had rolled up to court early only to find that his case had been adjourned and was in the office catching up on recent gossip when MacDonald had called. Alcock, remembering that the Cowboy had previously served in the court, called in a favour and so the Cowboy came to act as the prosecutor in a simple traffic case which was set for hearing that morning.

The defendant came from a well-heeled family that lived on the Peak and subscribed to the notion that traffic laws were not relevant to her luncheon expeditions, particularly when her driver was sick and she had to drive the Rolls Royce herself. In fact she had told the traffic constable as much when he had the temerity to pull her car over and summons her in the full view of her friends. The family solicitor, one Francis Ching, who normally concerned himself only with Contract and Tort had been summoned to attend court and ensure that justice was done.

The traffic constable entered the witness box and the Cowboy carefully led him through his evidence detailing the erratic manner in which the Rolls Royce had been driven on the day in question. The Cowboy paused, skimmed through his brief again, then looked up to the magistrate and indicated that the evidence was complete. The magistrate, smiling slightly, inquired if that was all the evidence and when the Cowboy replied in the affirmative, he turned to Ching and commented that he presumed Mr Ching wished to address the court.

Mr Ching shuffled the papers laid out on the counsel table then rose and addressing the constable put it to him that his client, the defendant, had not driven her car in the manner described. The constable, pointing towards the defendant, replied that she had so driven the car. At this point the magistrate could not hide a smile and with restrained irony thanked Mr Ching for assisting the prosecution by identifying the defendant to the court. There was a stunned silence, then the Cowboy mentally kicked himself for missing such a basic point in the evidence while Ching looked bemused, realizing that something had happened, but not sure just what so he continued with his cross examination. On the conclusion of the constable's evidence there was deemed to be a case to answer and the lady defendant entered the witness box. However, she clearly had no conception of what she was alleged to have done wrong and was highly indignant to be found guilty and fined a few hundred dollars. She sailed out of the court seething with injured innocence leaving Ching to settle the fine with the Court Shroff and then find his own way home.

The Smart Solicitor

Barnabus Gamble was a short, slightly overweight person with a very fair skin and a sparse auburn fringe around his bald head. He invariably dressed in loose fitting, light coloured suits, sported a club tie and even in the fiercest air conditioning perspired profusely. One cynic described him as a poor man's caricature of a Sidney Greenstreet character in a 'B' grade film.

However, Gamble was a long time resident of Asia and latterly of Hong Kong, hence he knew that the secret to success as a solicitor was to employ smart clerks who had good contacts and to be quick to take advantage of any opportunity afforded to him.

Whenever he appeared in court he would invariably approach the court prosecutor and discuss the case in an effort to ascertain the strength of the prosecution evidence and explore the potential for doing a deal whereby some charges were dropped in return for a guilty plea on other charges, or charges could be reduced to less serious ones in return for a guilty plea. At the same time his clerk, who modelled his appearance on a young Elvis Presley, was not averse to buying prosecution witnesses a coffee in the canteen in an attempt to glean additional information. The clerk also appeared to suffer from prostate problems particularly when defence witnesses were giving evidence and would politely 'greet' other witnesses as he entered and left the court room on his way to the toilet.

Prosecuting officers viewed the activities of Gamble and his clerk with a jaundiced eye and several lived to rue a casual, unguarded conversational remark which later came back to haunt them in open court. One day in the course of his cross examination Gamble displayed a deep knowledge of the prosecution evidence and it was only much later that the Cowboy remembered leaving his files on the counsel table when he went back to the office to make a telephone call. The possibility that Gamble had taken advantage of his absence to go through his case file grew into certainty the more he thought about it.

The Cowboy kept a careful eye on the Court Calendar during the following weeks and noted that Gamble was appearing for the defence in a drug trafficking case. The Cowboy prepared a duplicate case file but with slight alterations to the identifying particulars and some very significant amendments to the statement of the main witness.

On the morning of the hearing the Cowboy was in court early and shortly after Gamble arrived he made his excuses and left the court leaving the duplicate file on the counsel table. Some time later he returned carrying the genuine case file inside a copy of the *South China Morning Post* and when attention was diverted as the magistrate entered he swapped the files around.

On the conclusion of the evidence of the main witness Gamble rose and started to address the court on the ethics of officers of the court and commented that the prosecuting officer although not a fully qualified solicitor should also follow these ethics. He observed that it was the duty of the prosecuting officer to inform the court when a witness did not come up to brief as in the case before the court. The Cowboy, with an air of injured innocence, protested that the witness had come up to brief. Whereupon Gamble cited apparent disparities in the statement of the witness and the evidence given before the court.

The Cowboy sought, and was given approval, to produce the statement in question which, after the magistrate half glanced at it, was handed to Gamble. He looked at it then started to exclaim that it was not the same as . . . then paused and sat down. The magistrate realizing something was amiss asked Gamble for an explanation for his attack on the prosecution and when none was forthcoming took it upon himself to lecture Gamble on wasting the time of the court with groundless allegations. The Cowboy could scarcely contain his amusement nor could some of the other court prosecutors who had quietly entered the court room to listen to proceedings.

The defence folded and the case came to an abrupt ending when Gamble entered no defence other than a routine plea in mitigation blaming the defendant's behaviour on coming from a broken home and problems at school.

After the court rose the First Clerk informed the Cowboy that he was to present himself in the Magistrate's Chambers immediately. The magistrate was well aware that the Cowboy had pulled something on Gamble and demanded an explanation which the Cowboy provided. The magistrate took it in good humour but warned the Cowboy in no uncertain terms of the consequences if he ever again played such juvenile tricks in the court room.

Some months later Gamble again appeared in court representing a female who was charged with trafficking in dangerous drugs. The evidence was quite straightforward in that a police party had entered and searched the female's flat in the course of which several large packets of dangerous drugs were found stashed in a cupboard. On completion of the prosecution evidence Gamble, with a fine sense of drama, called an aged male into the witness box. The male who claimed to be over 70 years of age and a drug addict for over fifty years stated that he had visited the female defendant's flat some weeks previously and unbeknown to her had secreted the drugs in the flat for safety. The magistrate quite naturally dismissed the charges and ordered that the male be taken into custody and brought before him the following day on appropriate charges.

The Cowboy was well aware that the female defendant was a major figure in the street-level drug dealing in her area and was convinced that the evidence of the man was a fabrication. As he left the court room he asked the old man why he had taken the blame for the woman. To his surprise the man explained that he was a street sleeper faced with the onset of the cold winter months so he had accepted a cash offer from him, pointing towards the retreating back of Gamble's clerk, and claimed the latter had promised that the solicitor would, in view of the circumstances, get him only a token sentence.

The Cowboy was elated at the revelation and at the prospect of the old man repeating this story in court the following morning. He considered recording a formal statement from the old man but since the latter was illiterate and such statement would not be on oath he decided to let matters rest overnight and the man was escorted away for detention at the local police station.

The following morning the Cowboy was at court bright and early waiting for the prisoners to arrive. As soon as the prisoners were processed he took the old man to one side and told him that he wanted him to repeat his story of the previous evening to the magistrate in court. To his dismay the old man refused. It came out that Gamble's clerk had visited him in the police station cells the previous evening and warned him that he faced a long term of imprisonment if he admitted lying on oath to secure the release of the female defendant, whereas if he stuck with his story he would have the money and would only serve a short term of a few months.

The Cowboy cursed his own lack of foresight in not ensuring that the old man had been 'lost' in the cells of some other police station. He contemplated approaching the magistrate and explaining what had transpired but in discussion with fellow prosecutors it was felt that such action had no concrete evidence to support it and might be considered an attempt to influence the court. In any event, it would tend to compromise the integrity of the court. All the Cowboy could do was await the outcome of the morning's hearing and hope that the magistrate handed down a two or three year sentence.

The magistrate lauded the old man for his honourable

conduct and sense of civic responsibility in coming forward to save an innocent person from jail and in view of these mitigating circumstances, taking into account the age and history of the defendant, the magistrate sentenced him to a token three months in jail. The Cowboy almost choked suppressing his anger and personal outrage that Gamble, or at least his clerk, had got away with it. He could not resist the urge to confront the clerk with his knowledge but the clerk merely smiled and rubbed his thumb and first finger together then turned and sauntered off after Gamble.

Crime Does Not Pay

Harry Craggs was a big, bluff, overweight police officer whose career was going nowhere faster than the San Miguel flowed down his throat. In his time he had been a competent investigator but now he served as a court prosecutor to keep him out of harm's way until he took early retirement. In the mornings he was able to perform his duties but after his usual liquid lunch he became a liability so the unofficial duty of custody officer was created for him as it did not matter if he dosed off in the office chair – the NCO on cell duty would manage quite efficiently on his own. On his way home in the evenings Harry would stop off at the Police Sports Club or one of the police Messes for several hours before he staggered home to his patient wife. The wife was a local Chinese girl and his marriage was one of the reasons his police career came to an abrupt halt and he turned to alcohol to drown his sorrows.

Mrs Craggs was a petite woman who had been attractive in a blowzy fashion in her youth but, like many other neglected wives, she did not pay much attention to her dress or appearance and her whole life focused on her daughter who was the centre of her existence. As with many men who drink to drown their disappointment with life, there were occasions when Harry returned home under the influence and vented his frustration upon his patient wife. She had little choice but to endure the life – her own family had disowned her when she had disgraced them by marrying a 'Gwai Lo' (foreign devil).

One night Harry came home late after a heavy drinking session and started to complain about no meal waiting for him which led him to discover an even more serious matter, the absence of any cold beer in the fridge. In a rage he turned upon his wife and in his angry gesticulations he struck her several times. Something snapped her long held restraint and almost without realizing it she picked up a carving knife and plunged it into his ample midriff. As he sank to the floor and she stood over him with the bloodstained knife they both were in a state of shock and it was only when Harry cursed and asked what the hell she thought that she was doing that they both realized what had happened. Quickly she handed him a large dishcloth to staunch the wound then ran into the lounge and dialled 999 for assistance.

The ambulance was on the scene within three minutes and Harry was whisked away to hospital whilst the police escorted her back to Kowloon City Police Station for enquiries. On arrival Harry was examined by an intern who, detecting the strong aroma of alcohol, decided that Harry should sleep it off before he attended to the wound which seemed quite superficial. Three hours later Harry was dead as a result of internal haemorrhaging and two days later Mrs Craggs appeared in Magistrates' Court facing a murder charge.

Helen LO was the first female solicitor to open her own law practice in Hong Kong and later was the first female judge. Whilst she would be the first to dissociate herself with Woman's Liberation as such, she strongly advocated equal opportunity of education for daughters as well as sons. She was acutely conscious of the existing bias against women, particularly in the field of matrimonial matters in which she was becoming a specialist. When the case was brought to her attention she felt a considerable sympathy for Mrs Craggs as a battered wife long before such a term became politically correct. In her preparations for the trial she was assisted by two sympathetic police officers, Jim Curries and Mike Quinn, who provided her with significant background information.

The all male jury were sympathetic to the evidence adduced on behalf of Mrs Craggs and, despite directions from the judge, not only found her not guilty of murder but also not guilty of wounding and Mrs Craggs walked out of court a free woman.

A few weeks later Mrs Craggs came to see Helen LO again to seek assistance. The government Quartering Officer had ordered her eviction from the quarters she was occupying as she was no longer entitled to them. She was not in receipt of any pension, had no money and nowhere to go. As no conviction had been recorded, Helen LO felt that there were grounds for Mrs Craggs to receive her widow's pension and promptly sued Government for it. After some protracted negotiations the Government representatives conceded and Mrs Craggs started to receive her pension.

Now Helen LO was on full throttle and she promptly took out a writ for compensation against the Medical and Health Department on the grounds that prompt and efficient medical attention when Harry had first arrived at the hospital might have saved his life. Even more protracted negotiations took place but eventually the government Legal Department offered to settle out of court and Mrs Craggs received a substantial sum in compensation, certainly enough to ensure that the daughter was able to have a good education.

Chapter Four

LO HIN-SHING – DOYEN OF THE COURTS

L O Hin-shing, more frequently called Hin-Shing LO, was born in Hong Kong around 1890 and at the age of 5 went to China to study for the Imperial Examinations with a view to later obtaining an appointment from the Emperor of China. In 1905 the Emperor KWONG SHUI issued an edict abolishing the Imperial Examination and thus a tradition of over 1,300 years came to an end and a young boy's dreams were shattered.

Shortly afterwards Hin-Shing left his heung ha (native place) returned to Hong Kong and commenced a Western education with the result that he was among the first seventy-five students who were admitted to the newly established Hong Kong University in 1912 and was the first president of the Hong Kong University Students' Union. It was as a young student that Hin-Shing first became interested in horse racing but he could only afford to patronize the public stands and he developed a fierce envy of the members of the Jockey Club. One night as he made his way home early following poor choices of horses, he came upon a row of carriages waiting for their owners and to express his irritation he quietly opened each carriage door as he walked past and urinated on the floor inside.

Upon graduation Hin-Shing managed to obtain entry to Trinity Hall, Cambridge as a graduate of a junior affiliated institute to study for his Masters Degree in Law. However, he now needed a passport in order to travel to the United Kingdom and sought assistance from a fellow clansman who held high office under the Crown. An appointment was made for the pair to meet with His Excellency The Governor who took kindly to Hin-Shing and immediately authorized the issue of a new British passport. When he came to providing his personal particulars Hin-Shing was somewhat embarrassed at being still a student at over 30 years of age so taking advantage of his youthful appearance and the fact that to most Gwai Lo (foreign devils) all Chinese look alike, he took several years off his age. Later, on his death, this caused some difficulties as his family announced his death at the venerable age of 103 whereas the official government records showed him to be merely 99 years of age.

In October 1922 Hin-Shing passed his Bar Final Examinations and in January 1923 he was called to the English Bar under the sponsorship of Sir Edward Clark QC and Mr Travers Humphreys. However, his family considered that he would be more useful to the family interests as a solicitor rather than as a barrister so Hin-Shing commenced a short pupillage, under a Mr Goddard of Goddard and Company, Solicitors. The pupillage came to a swift termination after Mr Goddard decided that Hin-Shing was wasting his time roaming London and would be better employed as a barrister in Hong Kong. During the following years Hin-Shing continued to roam London and cut a somewhat unusual figure on the social scene of the time being Chinese, a respectable barrister and, apparently, of independent means.

He was invited to many soirees, formal functions and even one memorial day wangled an invitation to the Royal Box at Epsom for Derby Day. On such formal occasions guests were formally announced upon their arrival and Hin-Shing decided that plain Hin-Shing LO Esquire just did not have sufficient appeal so he styled himself His Highness The Prince of Shaukiwan after a small fishing village on Hong Kong Island and thereafter was announced as such on formal occasions. He continued to enjoy a good social life and learnt to excel at all the modern dances including the tango and this latter ability stood him in good stead when he eventually returned to Hong Kong.

In 1926 Hin-Shing returned to Hong Kong and practised as a barrister for the next twenty-odd years including the period of the Japanese Occupation of Hong Kong. In 1948 he was appointed as a police magistrate, a title dating back to 1841, and sat in the Central Magistracy which formed part of the Central Police Station. Sitting as a magistrate with Hin-Shing was another venerable Chinese magistrate called Freddie POON and they became great friends, enjoying a good social life together.

On one occasion the pair of them enjoyed a very convivial evening on the town and in the early hours of the morning found themselves on a deserted street and in urgent need of answering a call of nature. After looking around carefully the cheerful duo decided to unbutton their trousers at the entrance to a darkened doorway but to their great consternation the darkened recess was also the resting place of a pair of Hong Kong's Finest, who were not at all amused by their warm and wet awakening. The two officers of the court took a stand on their alcoholic dignity and were most adamant that justice must be done. Much to the distress of members of the local constabulary summonses were duly taken out against both offenders.

In the cold light of the following day consternation spread within a select circle including the two culprits and after much discussion it was decided that the summonses would be heard after the normal close of the Magistrates' Court with each culprit taking it in turn to sit as magistrate so that justice could at least appear to be done. Freddie POON sat first and Hin-Shing duly presented himself before the court, dutifully pleaded guilty and was fine $10. Court was adjourned and the pair reversed roles. Freddie POON pleaded guilty and Hin-Shing fined him $100 which provoked a protest from

POON at the size of the fine to which Hin-Shing replied that the offence was becoming far too prevalent and it was in fact the second such case before the court that day. Neither of the gentlemen was of such a character as to allow such trifles to interfere with friendship and they continued to enjoy life.

Late one afternoon one of them was hearing a series of minor hawking offences which were dragging on late into the day and he was in a hurry to get away. As the final papers were being cleared the court prosecutor asked for an Order in respect of the exhibits, a number of chickens in one case. The learned magistrate shuffled his papers in acknowledgement and shortly afterwards left the court to keep a pressing social engagement. The property constable, who arrived shortly afterwards, was rather put out on receiving the Court Papers to find that the chickens had been bound over to be of good behaviour. In the absence of any magistrate to amend the Court Order he could not return the chickens but had to tend to them overnight and seek a new Court Order the following morning.

On another occasion the pair of them went to a Chinese dance hall in the company of an aspiring young Eurasian barrister. Hin-Shing was in his element on these occasions as he was such an excellent dancer and frequently the ladies approached him for impromptu dancing lessons, which also meant that he enjoyed their company without having to pay for the 'dance hour'.

The young barrister was particularly taken with the attractions of one of the young ladies and since his Cantonese was a little rudimentary he solicited the sage advice of Hin-Shing on an appropriate but complimentary approach in Cantonese to the lady. Hin-Shing suggested that he tell the lady that she was most attractive and invite her to 'Tung kui hand lo' (walk the floor with him). This sounded suitable to the barrister who approached the lady and was immediately rewarded with a barrage of uncomplimentary aspersions on his birth. He returned crestfallen to his table where he found the pair convulsed in mirth. Unbeknownst to the poor barrister the suggested phrase was a less than polite local euphemism suggesting that the lady might care to sleep with him.

During the 1950s Magistrates' Courts were established at Western, Causeway Bay, South Kowloon, North Kowloon and Fanling in addition to the old court at Central. These courts served the police stations in their area and the magistrates soon came to know the police officers from these stations and the standard of their work. This judicial note by the magistrates was a little more obvious in some courts than in others and Hin-Shing was perhaps the most obvious of all the magistrates of the period.

On occasion Hin-Shing, when there was a more serious case, would enquire who was the officer-in-charge of the case and sometimes, irrespective of the plea by the defendant, he would enter a plea of not guilty and set a date to hear the evidence. At other times on learning the name of the officer-in-charge he would turn to the defendant and suggest that he did not waste the time of the court by pleading not guilty as this would only lead to a more severe sentence when he was found guilty.

Sometimes after hearing the evidence of a police officer that he knew and trusted he would turn to counsel for the defence and quietly suggest that it might be appropriate to seek new instructions from his client, implying that he was already satisfied that the defendant was guilty. Most counsel would follow the suggestion and on reversing their plea would be complimented on their sagacity which would be reflected in the sentence he would pronounce.

On more than one occasion he told a defendant that the police officer involved in the case would not have put the defendant in the dock if he were not guilty and warned him of the perils of wasting the court's time. On the other hand, after hearing the evidence he has turned to a defendant and stated that whilst he was convinced that the defendant was guilty the evidence was not strong enough and he acquitted such defendant with a warning not to come before him again on a similar charge.

Hin-Shing was an avid devotee of the 'Hong Kong Religion', known in other parts of the world as horse racing, and it is perhaps significant that his most outrageous remarks would come around noon on a Saturday when the racing commenced in the early afternoon. In modern days these strictures from the Bench would have evoked the wrath of the Appeal Court and indeed outrage the advocates of human rights. However, it must be recorded that in a total of over twenty-five years of dispensing justice in Magistrates' Courts he retired three times, the last time on his eight-first birthday – none of his decisions were ever overturned on appeal and Hin-Shing enjoyed a public recognition from all spheres of the private sector as a most honourable and just magistrate. This was a unique accolade in a society where the majority are taught from birth never to trust a 'koon' (official) as all were corrupt and dishonourable.

Chapter Five

CHARLES FFOUKES-SMYTHE

Commander Charles ffoukes-Smythe RN (Rtd) and his charming wife Barbara arrived in Hong Kong quietly one autumn and took up residence in spacious premises in Jardine's Lookout. He was in his early middle age and a barrister by profession, whilst Barbara, a few years his senior, came from what might be termed a good background in the United Kingdom.

A few months after his arrival he set up Chambers in Prince's Building in Central and astutely took on two recently qualified local barristers as his juniors. Dominic CHAU was the scion of a very wealthy Chiu Chow property developer and whilst not blessed with an overly developed intellect had extensive commercial and social connections throughout the Chiu Chow Community in Hong Kong. David CHAN on the other hand came from a less prosperous background, being the only son of a mini-bus driver and brought up in a low cost housing estate. However, he possessed a very sharp brain to support his burning ambition to achieve success. The chambers prospered although ffoukes-Smythe himself seldom appeared in court. He preferred to use his worldly charm to persuade litigants that settling matters out of court was preferable to taking a chance on the uncertainties of a hearing in open court with its attendant publicity.

In Hong Kong society a perceived image of wealth is essential for success and the ostentatious display of wealth is considered quite acceptable. One very socially acceptable couple called their house Villa D'Ora and everything in the house down to the bathroom fittings was gold plated. When Hagen Das Ice Cream was first introduced to Hong Kong it was marketed as the most expensive ice cream in the world and the police had to be called out to control the crowds thronging up to buy it.

Charles and Barbara acquired the trappings of wealth, including a Rolls Royce with liveried chauffeur, and slowly assumed the mantle of social lions. Scarcely a day went by without a photograph of one or the other appearing on the social pages of the local tabloids and they became accepted as being essential to the social recognition of any function. Charles was quite pedantic about the correct social etiquette and had been known to change his clothing six times in one day in order to be dressed appropriately for the occasion. Even on a stifling hot summer's day Charles would appear in his chambers dressed in his half-lined dark pin-striped suit with bowler and rolled umbrella in order to maintain the standards.

It was a simple matter of precedence that set in motion a train of events that led to the downfall of Commander Charles ffoukes-Smythe RN (Rtd).

Each year there is formal ceremony to celebrate the Opening of the Assizes, which in modern Hong Kong is something of an anachronism, attractive mainly to camera-toting tourists. Members of the Judiciary and of the legal profession don their traditional robes and finery complete with full-bottomed wigs, gowns, breeches and stockings, then parade in public. Charles had problems with his attire that morning which resulted in his being late leaving home and even later arriving for the ceremony. Instead of quietly taking a position at the rear of the assembled gentry, he pompously insisted on making his way to the front ranks to assume his appropriate position. Perhaps because it was a hot day and he felt uncomfortable, this grand entrance by Charles thoroughly irritated a fellow barrister and his feelings were not assuaged when Charles, instead of offering any apology, merely complained that no one had seen fit to reserve his position.

Gregory Dunstan, the barrister, decided that it was time that Charles was cut down to size and, on returning to his chambers, he contacted a firm of private detectives and tasked them with an investigation into Charles. Two months passed and the private detectives provided little of value for Dunstan so he decided to expand the scope of the investigation to the United Kingdom. A month later the report from the private detectives in the United Kingdom more than justified their expense as far as Dunstan was concerned.

According to the report Charles had served in the Royal Navy but far from being a dashing destroyer captain in the Mediterranean he had spent almost the entire war period as a supplies officer in a small depot in Scotland and had left the Royal Navy as Lieutenant Charles Smith, the ffoukes-Smythe being acquired at some later period. He had been a member of a large chambers in London but after some undisclosed problems had left the chambers and travelled the Country Court Circuit. There he had met Barbara, who had inherited a considerable fortune on the recent death of her husband. They had married after a whirlwind courtship, a union that did not meet with the approval of most of Barbara's social circle who suspected that Charles had married the older Barbara for her inheritance and were not slow in making their feelings apparent. After a few months the newly-weds had departed for Hong Kong to start a new life together. However, a check of the marriage registries failed to produce any record of the purported marriage. Dunstan could hardly contain his glee and spent the next two weeks gloating as he considered the various courses of action open to him.

First he wrote a personal letter to the Captain of HMS *Tamar* pointing out that Charles had not held the rank claimed. Furthermore, at Remembrance Day Ceremonies he had worn medals to which he was not entitled. Dunstan professed outrage at this insult to the 'Gallant Fallen' and demanded

48

that the Captain take action. He dispatched an edited version of the report anonymously to the editors of the local tabloids and of local society magazines. To seal his action, a copy of the report was passed to the Inland Revenue Department suggesting that Charles might have been claiming allowances for a wife when he was not legally married.

In a matter of days the whole world collapsed upon Charles starting with the posting of his dismissal on the notice board of the Officers' Mess in HMS *Tamar*, a request to visit the Investigation Section of the Inland Revenue Department and scurrilous articles appearing in the Chinese language press.

At first Charles tried to brazen out matters but the local community has no sympathy for those who fall off their pedestals. A month later, on grounds of failing health, Charles announced his retirement from practice and his imminent departure for the more peaceful environment of Cyprus. His farewell party was the social event of the year with over a hundred uninvited guests and scores of reporters in attendance.

Chapter Six

DISTRICT VICE SQUAD

In April 1965 the Cowboy returned from vacation leave in the United Kingdom and, having attended a CID course at the Metropolitan Police Detective Training School in Chelsea, he anticipated a posting to a CID formation. On arrival, he found that he was posted to Uniform Branch at Hong Kong Island District Headquarters and in fact throughout the rest of his career he never again served in CID.

He hung around the Headquarters for several days but no one seemed to know what was being lined up for him and he made it a point of principle not to try to manoeuvre any particular post since this only left one under an obligation.

One morning Chris Dawson, Assistant Commissioner in Command of Hong Kong Island District, summoned the Cowboy to his office. Dawson had decided to establish a special new District Vice Squad which would be drawn from inspectorate officers who had recently graduated from the Police Training School and the Cowboy was to command the new squad. Aside from being targeted against gambling, prostitution and dangerous drugs the squad would also serve as a training ground for the new inspectorate officers and on return to their divisions they could take command of the local vice or drug squads. Each attachment to the squad would be for twenty-seven days so that the officers would not be entitled to plain clothes allowance for which there was a twenty-eight day minimum period.

Dawson, known to all as Chi Sing Ma (Crazy Horse), was very enthusiastic about his new young officer's squad and intended to use it to keep the divisions up to the mark. If the new squad seized more than two opium pipes in a divan, arrested more than twenty persons in a gambling raid or seized more that 1,000 dollars in a gambling raid then the Divisional Superintendent would be called to account. Dawson assured the Cowboy that he would have full backing, but the Cowboy was a little dubious and he could foresee potential problems.

The Cowboy was assigned the vacant communications room in the basement, adjacent to the emergency control room where with eight telephones at least he had no communications problems. He was granted his request for two weeks for preparation and set about organizing himself. He acquired large full-scale maps of the Island and using the daily crime reports over the previous three months he marked all the drug arrests with pins. A dozen little clusters of pins gathered on the maps and the Cowboy now knew the approximate location of all the heroin stalls on the Island.

The Force was very statistics oriented so the divisional drug squads contented themselves with arresting two or three addicts each day and thus maintained their figures. If they arrested the actual dealers or forced the dealers to move on then they faced a barren period with no arrests, resulting in harassment from senior officers for doing nothing.

Having identified the approximate locations, the Cowboy visited the areas after dark and prowled around until he found a lone Doh Yau (drug addict) whom he would take into custody. The Doh Yau was searched and if drugs were found on him he was given the choice of being taken back to the station and charged, or giving the Cowboy full details of where he had purchased his drugs including size of operation, terms used in making purchases and any precautions taken by the dealers. Occasionally if the search produced nothing the Cowboy would produce simulated packets from his pockets and use these to intimidate the Doh Yau into providing the information. It was perhaps an indictment of the Force that the Doh Yaus never doubted that the Cowboy would frame them in this manner. However, the Cowboy felt that the ends justified the means even if the odd Doh Yau was released when there were grounds to charge him.

The CID monthly intelligence reports gave the locations used as illegal casinos but these operations were usually very mobile and often employed a sophisticated system of alarms. The reports were also somewhat misleading in that the Chinese count the ground floor as one, against the Western custom of ignoring the ground floor. There were added complications in that a Chinese officer might convert his count to conform to the Western reckoning for the benefit of a senior European officer, who in turn would also convert the figure, and, of course, vice versa so that any address could end up two or three floors out in the final report. Jock Atkinson in CID Eastern came up with the best system as his reports gave 'Lift Button Numbers' but the other officers would not fall in line with this practice.

The Cowboy was not a gambler because he was a bad loser so he really knew little about gambling and realized that if he was to take gambling cases to court he had better acquire some expertise. He was lucky in that FUNG Loi the officer-in-charge of the Island anti-Triad Squad was an expert in this field and was willing to take the time to teach the Cowboy and also to give up one day each month to teach each new squad. FUNG Loi explained the main local games of chance.

Fan Tan

A pile of porcelain buttons or counters are covered under a container and the punters wager on the numbers one to four. When the bets are closed the banker counts out the counters on groups of four until only one to four are left to produce the winning number. Wagers can also be made on odd or even numbers. The winner on a single number gets twice the amount staked whilst on combination wagers the winning is evens.

Yu Ha Hai

The six faces of the dice feature Yu (fish), Ha (crab), Hai (prawn), Gaai (cockrel), Woo Lo (beet) and Kam Tsin (coin). Three dice are shaken inside a container, often a bowl in a saucer, and punters wager on what will be shown. One feature gives evens, two features twice the stake and three features three times the stake.

Taai Sai

Three dice are shaken inside a container and punters wager on the total number to be shown on the dice when uncovered. If the total is three or eighteen the bank wins. Wagers can also be laid on whether the total will be Sai (small) between four and ten or Taai (big) between eleven and seventeen. The returns on individual numbers vary in rough proportion to the chances of the number coming up whilst wagers on Taai or Sai pay evens.

Tse Fa

This is a simple form of lottery in which the punter selects two numbers between one and thirty-six and the winning numbers pay a specified dividend depending upon the size of the lottery. The lottery is usually operated on a local basis and there could even be separate lotteries in adjacent streets. However, since the twice-daily draw is conducted in private the choice of winning numbers is often not left to chance but the least popular combination is selected by the operators.

Doh Ma

Doh Ma (bookmaking) is a major concern and the legal bookmaking on the Royal Hong Kong Jockey Club Tote is one of the biggest bookmaking operations in the world. However, gambling was only permitted within the racecourse on race days until the seventies when off-course betting centres were opened by the Jockey Club in an effort to reduce the extent of illegal operations. Prior to that the illegal bookmaking was an extensive and very lucrative business with large sophisticated concerns operating out of private premises with up to twenty telephone lines, each equipped with tape recorders, and a race day turnover of several million dollars down to the small time street corner bookmaker with a turnover of a few hundred dollars.

During the period that the Cowboy was preparing for the squad to become operational he became aware that the new squad was the subject of much speculation among some colleagues and a few of his closer acquaintances warned him obliquely of the potential dangers if he upset the 'system' too much, though no one came out openly and make any specific threats. It was a typically Chinese-style approach to negotiate through intermediaries until a solution was reached, then to make a formal proposal. With a squad of inspectorate officers who had just left the Police Training School the Cowboy realized that he had no choice but to play it straight and there was no way to avoid a confrontation within CID. Indirectly, he sent this message back to CID and the only compromise he could offer was to avoid hitting any one station too often and raiding the same area more than once each day. Strangely, this was apparently acceptable but the Cowboy was warned that all activities inside the Happy Valley Racecourse were the personal bailiwick of LUI Lok, Staff Sergeant Class I of CID Hong Kong Island and that he crossed LUI at his peril.

The Cowboy was aware that there was an extensive illegal bookmaking operation conducted within the racecourse and strongly suspected that some Jockey Club officials were involved, even facilitating the operation by providing race day badges for the illegal bookmakers. Major wagers were frequently made in the members' stands and even in the private boxes used by stewards and other officials. Fortunately, there was only one race meeting each week during the season so, although Dawson urged him to take action, he was able to stall for some time by just keeping observation. This proved quite beneficial in that after some of the groups were identified the Cowboy noticed that there were often heavy betting plunges just before the start of a race when one of the groups was laying off bets. By simply following this he was able to make his own small wagers. Over the season he doubled his monthly salary by this simple expedient.

Eventually, the Cowboy was forced to make a move and three persons were arrested for accepting bets in the members' stand and taken to Causeway Bay Magistrates' Court where they appeared before Mr O'Connor. He held that the members' stand was a private place requiring the authority of a gambling warrant to effect arrests therein and he released the defendants.

A few weeks later the Cowboy, now armed with a gambling warrant issued by Dawson, arrested three more persons for accepting bets and once again they appeared before Mr O'Connor. This time he held that pursuant to the provisions of the Gambling Ordinance the execution of a gambling warrant required the Cowboy to arrest and detain all the persons found gambling on the premises. He further questioned the validity of the gambling warrant since the premises in question were licensed for gambling. The Cowboy was happy to compile a full report then pass it to Dawson who then referred it to the government Legal Department and that was the last the Cowboy heard about the problem of gambling within the Jockey Club, much to his relief.

Prostitution in itself was not illegal in Hong Kong and the principal related offences were soliciting for an immoral purpose, living on immoral earnings, controlling the movements of a prostitute and keeping a brothel.

A brothel was defined as any premises habitually used by two or more females for the purposes of prostitution. Technically, many of the bars and dance halls in Hong Kong were brothels but it would have taken considerable time and effort to obtain the evidence necessary to secure a conviction. In any event it did not present sufficient of a problem to justify the effort. In addition, there were a number of Yat Lau Yat Fong (one flat one phoenix) or one-girl establishments particularly in Jaffee Road which technically did not breach the law.

There were a number of apartment houses or guest houses which specialized in hiring out their rooms for 'short periods' and after a guest had checked in the prostitutes would be summoned to the premises. In order to keep them in check, the police made regular visits and only occasionally mounted an operation against them. The military authorities in Hong Kong operated a small combined services squad which visited the bars regularly and checked that all girls on the premises visited the social hygiene centres or a private doctor at least once a week for a check up and records were maintained of these visits on 'blue cards'. If the squad found any girls without cards or with outdated cards then the bar was placed out of bounds to servicemen for a period of up to a month, which caused the proprietors a significant loss of revenue.

The combined efforts did nothing to curtail prostitution but served to keep it within bounds and prevent any major abuses. In respect of the apartment houses and guest houses the Cowboy imposed his own rules in that if the proprietor retained more than twenty-five per cent of the fee then he would increase the frequency of 'visits' which disrupted proceedings and caused a loss of revenue, but if the twenty-five per cent rate was maintained then the visits were seldom more than monthly. When the squad commenced operations many of the proprietors were retaining in excess of sixty per cent of the fee but within six months most were in line. The Cowboy took some satisfaction from this success which incidentally produced an additional bonus in that several of the prostitutes quietly passed on information to the Cowboy concerning drugs and gambling. During the fourteen months the Cowboy was in command of the District Vice Squad only ten squads were operational as the Star Ferry Riots of 1966 caused an hiatus.

Initially, most of the young Chinese inspectors were apprehensive about their ability to purchase drugs at street stalls so in the early period of each squad the Cowboy would chose a small stall which was operated in a poorly illuminated site such as a rear staircase of an old tenement building or rear alley. With his acquired knowledge of the terms in use he would purchase a few packets of drugs. In Western District the terms used were 'Tin' (sky), 'Dei' (ground) and 'Yan' (man) referring to No 4 heroin, No 3 heroin and baritone respectively. These terms also had Triad connotations since the word 'triad' derives from the 'Society of Earth, Sky and Man'.

The first time he brought a dealer arrested in such circumstances before Mr O'Connor the learned magistrate refused to accept a plea of guilty as he could not believe that a Gwai Lo (foreigner) would be able to buy drugs in such a manner. The dealer explained that the Cowboy was tall and spoke Cantonese with a northern accent so he had assumed that he was from Shanghai.

On one occasion the squad took up position on the rooftop of a school in Shaukeiwan and watched a dealer in operation in the street below. As each transaction was made the dealer would take his stock from inside the bumper of an adjacent parked lorry and hand packets to the purchaser, then pass the money to a second man. After watching several transactions, one inspector went down and successfully purchased two packets and returned to the roof-top.

It should have been a simple case, but as the officers moved in across the school compound they were observed and everyone scattered with the officers in chase. The dealer and the second man were both caught after chases along the street but on returning to the site there were no drugs to be found in the bumper of the lorry. It was difficult to proceed on a charge of dealing, with only two packets of drugs as evidence. Luckily, the magistrate accepted the evidence of the observation plus the actual purchase with marked money and both went down for three years. The Cowboy learned to plan a little better in future and thereafter one officer was always briefed to ignore bodies and go for the drugs.

Kong Sin Wan (Telegraph Bay) only had one narrow access road which wended around the top of the valley before descending into the bay thus those near the shore had ample warning of the approach of any police party. It was reported that a successful opium divan operated in the pigsties near the foreshore so the Cowboy decided to approach at dusk from the sea. A colleague, Mike Duggan, was a keen sailor and owned a small converted Chinese junk and agreed to take the squad in by sea and drop them off near the entrance to the bay.

All went to plan and the officers plunged into the sea about thirty yards from the headland and swam around it whilst the junk turned about and sailed away. On rounding the headland, the squad found yet another headland 100 yards further on and realized that they had been dropped off well short of the designated location. However, faced with steep rocky cliffs there was no alternative but to swim on. Eventually, five very tired officers crawled up the foreshore of Telegraph Bay and although the divan was only about thirty yards away none had the energy to tackle the addicts as they scattered. In the end the raid only produced one arrest, one opium pipe and a score of opium pots barely worth the effort. The Cowboy often wondered if Duggan had genuinely made an error of navigation in the dusk or had a perverse sense of humour.

A gambling establishment on the seventeenth floor of the Phoenix Apartments gained the reputation of being the 'Iron House'. Though police parties raided it frequently, they could never get past the system of watchers and the three iron gates that guarded the entrance in time to prove that gambling had been taking place. No gaming exhibits would be found inside the premises though chips and other paraphernalia might be found subsequently in the street below and the occupants would claim they were meeting for a social occasion.

After a number of unsuccessful attempts the squad infiltrated the building during the morning and holed up in a guest house for the rest of the day. Shortly before midnight the squad moved out. Using the rear staircase, they ascended to the seventeenth floor and prepared to carry out a raid. One officer managed to get through the outer iron grille but the inner grilles were secured in time. However, the occupant of the adjacent flat opened his door to see what was happening and the Cowboy brushed past him without ceremony and dashed into the bathroom which, luckily, was vacant at the time. He opened the bathroom window and in the airshaft outside was a metal frame used by the occupants to hang out their washing.

He did not pause but scrambled out onto the two-inch wide frame and walked along it to the adjacent bathroom window of the gambling establishment, unlatched the window and stepped in just as one of the operators rushed in with the intention of flushing some of the gambling sheets down the toilet. The man's face was a real picture of amazement, horror and fear when the Cowboy appeared out of mid air and threw him back whence he had come. Fortunately, three other officers had followed the Cowboy and it was a matter of seconds to secure the stunned occupants of the room.

None could believe what had happened and several, in the course of the next hour, went to the bathroom to see for themselves just how the officers had gained entry. When dawn broke and the officers saw how precarious was the metal frame, and looked down into the air shaft at the gathering rubbish some seventeen floors below, they tended to agree with the gamblers that it was crazy.

News of these exploits spread among the gambling and drug fraternities and all thought the Vice Squad officers were out of their minds. As it happened the film *633 Squadron* was enjoying a vogue in Hong Kong at that time so the Vice Squad acquired the sobriquet '633 Kam Sze Doi' (633 Death Defying Squad). The Reform Club of Hong Kong under the chairmanship of Brooke Berancci, a leading barrister, issued a confidential report based on privately commissioned research into vice in Hong Kong and the sobriquet gained official recognition when it appeared in the report which, among its many conclusions, commented that the most effective and feared anti-vice unit in Hong Kong was the 633 Squad. Dawson took great pleasure in this tribute to his 'Young Officer's Squad' and even took the current squad out for dinner on the strength of it.

During the Star Ferry Riots in the summer of 1966 the squad was suspended and the Cowboy hung around Headquarters doing odd jobs. Dawson became concerned that with the absence of a police presence on the streets gambling and drugs would start to proliferate, so one evening he ordered Hawker Smith, Divisional Superintendent of Western Division, to take his riot company out for a sweep through the division. The Cowboy paid little attention and continued reading his novel until Dawson turned to him and indicated that they were going out to check on the sweep and the Cowboy was to lead the way to known gambling sites to see if it was effective.

As Dawson was buckling on his Sam Browne belt the Cowboy sneaked a look at the controller's log and saw that the company's last reported position was in Sands Street in Kennedy Town. This area frequently appeared in the daily reports for drug and gambling arrests so the Cowboy thought it would be a good location to take Dawson and accordingly directed the driver of the Land Rover to Sands Street.

The Land Rover turned into the small square which harboured a small street market and to his horror the Cowboy saw a large gambling stall in full operation in the corner of the square. Naturally, the gamblers scattered in every direction but the occupants of the Land Rover, including the driver, all managed to arrest at least one gambler and recovered the scattered exhibits. Several thousand dollars had been collected. Dawson was enraged and sent a radio message for Smith and his senior officers to report to the scene immediately. Some fifteen minutes elapsed, during which Dawson became even more outraged, then Smith and his men arrived and Dawson gave them a severe dressing down.

The Cowboy could not understand what had happened and eventually asked one of the inspectors. A little reluctantly the officer recounted that the officers had taken some women constables up to the Inspectors' Mess and were having a party when the order had been received to carry out the sweep. Rather than break up the party someone had brought a Westminster Packset up to the Mess and the party had continued, with regular pauses for fictitious reports to be sent back on the Packset. The Cowboy was relieved to hear this information since he was not responsible for bringing the wrath of Dawson down upon the officers. It was their own fault for trying to be too clever.

A few days later Dawson came into the control room again and commanded the Cowboy and a couple of other officers to accompany him on another patrol of Western. As before, the Cowboy was to direct the driver to various known locations for street gambling. Following various circuitous routes, the party visited about half a dozen locations, all of which were quiet. This was not surprising since most stalls opened up in the evening when people had finished work for the day. After a fruitless hour of patrol Dawson directed that the party should proceed to Western Police Station and the Cowboy pointed out a location in a rear alley some hundred yards from the station.

The party alighted in Queen's Road West and walked down

61

a side street into the alley and found a sheet of tarpaulin blocking the way. Dawson stepped forward and, on pulling the tarpaulin aside, found four tables of 'Fan Tan' in progress. He immediately shouted that no one was to move and all were under arrest whilst the Cowboy and the other officers took cover in anticipation of what was going to happen. A human wave of about 200 persons surged forward and engulfed Dawson who was swept away and knocked to the ground. The other officers each grabbed a selected target, usually one of the bankers in order to gain the proceeds as well as making an arrest.

In the meantime Dawson brandishing a small wooden stool chased after the fleeing gamblers and ran out into Queen's Road West, where in frustration he threw the stool after the retreating backs. Unfortunately, his aim was not very good and the stool crashed through the windscreen of a car being driven along the road by a respectable businessman. When confronted by the dishevelled Dawson the driver thought discretion the better part of valour and drove on. Dawson sent another radio message summoning Smith and his senior officers then returned to the alley where the Cowboy and the other officers were sorting out the exhibits. When Smith and his men arrived Dawson again laid into them much to the embarrassment of the Cowboy and it did not help when Dawson left him in the station on his own to sort out the paperwork. Feeling like the proverbial pig in a synagogue, he doubted if anyone would give him a sheet of toilet paper if he asked for it.

The following morning the Cowboy was summoned to Headquarters and on arrival was informed that a formal complaint had been lodged against him in respect of the malicious damage to the windscreen of a car and it was possible that he would face criminal charges as a result of his irresponsible cowboy-like activities. Quickly realizing what it was all about, the Cowboy played along for a few minutes then pointed out that he was not the culprit and that it was Mr Dawson, Assistant Commissioner of Police, about whom the officer was talking. The interview was very abruptly terminated and the Cowboy heard no more about the incident.

Finally, it was time for a change. The Cowboy did not relish the prospect of serving in one of the divisions in which he had been operating. Dawson, shrewd enough to see this, did not let the Cowboy off the hook immediately. Only on the last morning was the Cowboy told he was to receive a Commendation and transfer to the Anti-Corruption branch.

Chapter Seven

THE DOWNFALL OF SOLICITOR TANG

The twenty years following the Japanese Occupation of Hong Kong was a period of reconstruction and a new Hong Kong grew out of the shambles that existed at the end of the war. An influx of refugees from the new Communist regime in China provided a work force, though many of the early refugees, particularly those from Shanghai, managed to bring substantial wealth with them. In the boom that followed many shrewd entrepreneurs made and sometimes lost vast fortunes. In 1970 it was claimed that Hong Kong had more first generation millionaires than anywhere else in the world. Wealth was to be flaunted and orders flowed for Rolls Royce and the other impedimenta of extravagance.

In this environment obtaining a professional qualification particularly a certificate to practise as a solicitor was, according to some cynics, a licence to print money. An appreciable number of the existing solicitors firms in Hong Kong were family concerns with two or three generations working in the same office and many close relatives in the same profession working in other offices so that there was an almost incestuous relationship between these firms. The driving ambition of the younger generation was to obtain professional qualifications and acquire the wealth and status that was there for the taking. It is small wonder that parents made many sacrifices to finance the education of their male children possibly looking on it as an investment for their own old age.

TANG Hon-tsai had a burning ambition to become a solicitor and, although not the most intelligent of his generation, he drove himself through his studies to achieve his ambition. It took him five attempts before he passed his Law Society Qualifying Examinations and at last was able to establish his law practice. He was soon earning a good income and able to purchase a fine home for his parents and start to enjoy the fruits of his diligence. As one of the new generation of professionals coming from a less advantaged background he became involved in the embryonic political movements in Hong Kong which sought to introduce social reform. He was a founder member and subsequently the chairman of the Hong Kong Labour Party and frequently helped organize petitions and small public protests outside Central Government Offices in Lower Albert Road on such issues as taxation, democracy and police powers. As a bachelor in his early thirties earning a good income, he enjoyed the night life offered by Hong Kong. He was a well known figure in the night-clubs and ballrooms particularly those on Hong Kong Island.

In Hong Kong, premises were licensed as dance halls and employed hostesses to entertain and dance with the customers who were charged for the privilege. These fees were known as 'dance hours' and varied according to the status of the establishment. At the top were the prestigious Oriental Ballroom in Mongkok and the Tonnochy Ballroom in Wanchai which catered for the wealthy of Hong Kong and employed the most attractive young ladies available.

In those days members of the Hong Kong Jockey Club took the issue of ladies' badges quiet literally and often engaged their partners for a day at the races from the ranks of the hostesses from the Oriental and Tonnochy Ballrooms. There were a number of lesser establishments, particularly in Kowloon, which catered for the less well off and a number of dark, dingy little establishments referred to in the local vernacular as Yu Daan Dong (fishball stalls) about which the less said the better. One of the dance hall licence conditions was that no alcohol was permitted to be served on the premises. However, the cold liquid poured from the china teapots often bore a very close resemblance to brandy.

CHAN Ming-chu was born just before the Japanese Occupation of Hong Kong in 1941, whilst her younger brother and sister were born after the Liberation of Hong Kong in 1945. Her father worked as a labourer with a small construction company and her mother was employed on piece rate in a plastics factory. At an early age she was forced to give up her schooling to join her mother in the factory as all the family finances were reserved for the education of the son. She was only 15 when she became pregnant following a casual relationship with a fellow factory worker many years her senior and the birth of a daughter caused a major rift in the family.

As a result CHAN moved out to fend for herself and her young child. She was not beautiful in the classical sense but had a good figure and the native intelligence to match it so she took the name KAM Lei and became a hostess in a small dance hall. As she matured and acquired greater street cunning she moved up the social dance hall ladder until she moved to the Plaza Dance Hall in Wanchai. Her ambition was to become a singer in one of the night-clubs or dance halls but this required finances and, if possible, a rich patron.

The evening of 10th December 1966 had been little different to many previous evenings when TANG had done the rounds of the dance halls and night-clubs. When he had arranged to meet KAM Lei for siu yeh (supper) after she had finished work that evening he had not anticipated that the minx would turn up together with her 6-year-old daughter. KAM claimed that it was the daughter's birthday so he had felt obliged to give KAM some money to buy a present for the girl. Looking at KAM as she sat in the passenger seat beside him with the child on her lap, he once again wondered just how old she was. She only looked about 20 in the soft reflection of the street lights.

The roads were quite deserted at that time in the morning and as he drove out of Jardine's Bazaar he made a fateful decision that was to lead him down a six-month-long convoluted path into disgrace. TANG decided to ignore the traffic sign prohibiting a right turn and turned right across Hennessey Road into Yee Woo Street to save time in order that he might get to one of the night-clubs before they closed at 2 am. Unfortunately, Police Constable 7175 saw the manoeuvre and stepping into the street signalled TANG to pull over. The constable pointed out the offence and requested that TANG produce his driving licence for inspection.

TANG was inclined to be a little arrogant at the best of times and to be treated in such a cavalier fashion by a mere constable in the presence of a hostess was loss of face. He alighted from the car and identified himself as TANG Lut-sze (solicitor TANG) and lectured the constable on the proper way to perform his duties, which did not include harassing a person of his status which amounted to an abuse of power. A patrolling sergeant came on the scene and he, too, became the subject of TANG's berating, much to the amusement of the gathering crowd. KAM Lei, at the suggestion of TANG, slipped away into the night with her daughter.

At this time the Cowboy was in command of the Hong Kong Island District Vice Squad and the squad had just come off a long, unproductive tour of duty. On their way to the Hung Uk (Red House), a late night restaurant in Percival Street, they came across the crowd and decided to see what was amiss.

The constable recognized the Cowboy and rapidly related what had happened so the Cowboy thought to settle matters quickly and then get on his way for a meal. Unfortunately, TANG had by this time worked himself into an indignant rage and when the Cowboy suggested that he simply resolve the matter by producing his driving licence, which was clearly visible in his shirt pocket, it only provoked a further outburst from TANG. TANG claimed that the police officers were humiliating him in public and that he should be treated with deference according to his status as a solicitor and an officer of the court. It did not help matters when the Cowboy retorted that he might try acting accordingly. At this point TANG discovered his pen was missing from his shirt pocket and claimed that the police sergeant had stolen it and should be arrested and searched.

The Cowboy felt that the situation was getting out of control and by now one of Hong Kong's famous instant crowds numbering over 100 had gathered at the scene. He suggested that everyone should adjourn to the then Eastern Police Station and conduct the affair privately but the more that the Cowboy emphasized the term 'sir' in reference to him the more TANG became outraged. Eventually, the Cowboy made it clear that if TANG did not accept the invitation then he would be arrested and there were seven officers at the scene.

On reaching the station TANG repeated his allegation that the sergeant had stolen his pen and in an attempt to defuse the situation the Cowboy apologized to the sergeant and conducted a quick search which he hoped would satisfy TANG. It was no avail and TANG continued to complain about harassment and abuse of police powers. He demanded his right to make a phone call and was permitted to use the phone in the report room. After talking agitatedly on the phone for several minutes TANG summoned the Cowboy and thrust the phone at him. The voice on the other end identified the speaker as Geoffrey Shears, a well-known barrister, who demanded that TANG be allowed to leave the station forthwith or a call would be made to the Commissioner of Police who was a personal friend.

The Cowboy had been considering the whole affair as a storm in a teacup which would blow over quickly. However, at this juncture he decided that it had gone too far so he invited the caller to do as he pleased and put the phone down. He formally placed Tang under arrest and escorted him to the detention cage adjacent to the report room.

The rest of the squad and the two Uniformed Branch officers were directed to go to the general office and record full details of the affair in their official notebooks, whilst he dealt with the paper work. The Cowboy prepared charges of disorderly conduct, disobeying a traffic sign, failing to produce a driving licence, assault (the Cowboy still had the imprint marks on his forearm where TANG had gripped him at one stage) and criminal damage (arising from TANG knocking a typewriter to the floor on his way to the phone). The charges were formally put to Tang and then the Cowboy arranged for TANG to be bailed out in the sum of one dollar to appear in court later that morning.

The Cowboy had barely an hour's sleep before the telephone burst into continuous life as everyone from the Attorney General to Chris Dawson, the Assistant Commissioner in command of Hong Kong Island District, wanted to know the full details of the affair. Dawson referred to a confrontation between himself and TANG outside the Ivory Tower (Central Government Offices) a few weeks previously so the case was of personal as well as professional interest to him. It was only then that it really dawned on the Cowboy that he had stirred up a hornets' nest and that if he were not careful he might end up being stung.

It was too late to halt the court proceeding which was the Cowboy's intention in bailing out TANG to appear in the Magistrates' Court later the same morning. When TANG appeared in court the last two charges were dropped and he entered pleas of 'not guilty' to the remaining three charges. The Cowboy felt that this was a tactical error but was overruled. The case was set for hearing the following week before Mr Hin-sing LO in Causeway Bay Magistracy, which was perhaps unfortunate for TANG as the magistrate had formed a favourable opinion of the Cowboy who had

69

frequently appeared before him.

The police witnesses gave their evidence. Mr LO held that there was a case to answer and adjourned the case to the following month to allow counsel to prepare the defence. On 14th March 1967 TANG gave his evidence which focused on the foul and abusive language that he claimed was used by the police officers and which his counsel said was more likely to have created a breach of the peace than anything that TANG might have done. In support of TANG, a female called LEUNG Suk-fan was called to the witness box. She claimed to have been the female passenger in the car at the time of the incident and, in a hesitant and highly embarrassed manner, also gave evidence of the alleged foul and abusive language used by the police officers.

At the end of the day the case was adjourned for another month and as the officers left the court the constable approached the Cowboy and stated that LEUNG was not the passenger in the car and that it had been a hostess called KAM Lei. He was quite positive about his recognition of KAM Lei since a couple of years previously, before she had become more popular and moved to the Plaza Dance Hall, he had enjoyed her favours several times.

The Cowboy reported this development to Chris Dawson and was directed to drop everything and concentrate on locating KAM Lei. The following evening the Cowboy took his squad to the Plaza Dance Hall to enquire about KAM Lei but the manager was most uncooperative, to the extent of claiming that he had never heard of KAM Lei even though her name appeared on the 'menu' of hostesses employed there.

The Cowboy decided to carry out a licence check on the premises which disrupted business for over half an hour. The squad left and took coffee for an hour in a nearby cafe then went back to the dance hall. Once again the manager was most uncooperative, so once again the Cowboy directed that a licence check be carried out. He apologized to the manager for disrupting business but pointed out that the dance hall was the only contact he had for KAM Lei and since it was imperative that he find her he would continue visiting until he did find her. A further hour was spent in the nearby cafe and the squad yet again visited the dance hall. This time the manager was waiting for them with a piece of paper in his hand on which was an address.

The Cowboy told the rest of the squad to go home and accompanied by a Chinese inspector went to the address at Prospect Mansion in Patterson Street. A teenage girl answered the door but when asked, stated that KAM Lei had moved away so the Cowboy thanked her and started to make for the lifts. As they waited a young female came out of the flat dressed in a blue baby-doll nightie and on approaching them said that she was KAM Lei. When asked she admitted that she knew Solicitor TANG and on further questioning she recalled being in a car with him a few nights before Christmas when he had been stopped by the police in Yee Woo Street. At his request she recorded these facts briefly in Chinese characters in the Cowboy's official notebook and was thanked for her assistance.

When the Cowboy reported his success the following morning Dawson was extravagant in his praise and directed that KAM Lei should be interviewed by a senior Chinese CID officer and a fully detailed statement recorded from her. Accordingly, arrangements were made for Superintendent CHAN Bing-wing to accompany the Cowboy to KAM Lei's flat that afternoon.

Unbeknown to the police officers Tang had been alerted to the police search for KAM Lei by the manager of the Plaza Dance Hall and had contacted her earlier that morning. When the two officers visited KAM she recanted her statement of the previous night claiming that it had been dictated to her by the Cowboy. At the request of CHAN she came to District Police Headquarters later that afternoon in the company of

TUNG Chi-keung, her 'kap lik' (a very close friend or pimp) and a solicitor's clerk. KAM again declined to make a formal statement but the visit did provide the constable and the sergeant with an opportunity to make a positive identification of KAM as the passenger in TANG's car.

The following morning the Cowboy went to the court early and obtained a witness summons requiring KAM Lei to appear in court to give evidence but on arrival at the flat in Prospect Mansion he discovered the premises vacant and learnt that KAM had moved out during the night. In the absence of KAM the hearing concluded and to the great relief of the Cowboy, Mr LO Hin-shing found TANG guilty as charged and fined him a total of $450.

Dawson was satisfied that TANG had committed perjury in the Magistrates' Court and was determined to bring TANG to trial on more serious charges. He convened a conference in his office and directed that CHAN Bing-wing should commence an investigation with this objective in mind. The address given in the Magistrates' Court by LEUNG Suk-fang was quickly found to be fictitious and a check of all females of that name in Hong Kong proved fruitless. A month went by but no trace could be found of KAM Lei and no leads were forthcoming from any of the dance halls so LUI Lok was briefed to make enquiries.

It was common knowledge that most of the vice activities – drugs, prostitution and gambling – in Hong Kong at that time were under the control of persons from Chiu Chow, a county in Southern Guangdong Province. It was equally true that most of the senior CID non-commissioned officers were also natives of Chiu Chow County and by tradition all persons from the same native place in China considered themselves to be 'brothers'. LUI Lok held the rank of staff sergeant class I in the Hong Kong Island CID and, therefore, was reputed to be a very powerful and influential figure. LUI quickly established a source of information in TANG's office by

72

recruiting the services of HUI Chi-wing, a young clerk who also happened to come from Chiu Chow County.

It was discovered that, at TANG's instigation KAM Lei had moved to the Portuguese Colony of Macau and was now working as a hostess over there. LUI Lok dispatched a 'ma tsai' (a little horse or follower) to Macau to confirm the information and if it was correct to advise the 'brothers' over there that their 'Big Brother' LUI would very much appreciate her returning voluntarily to Hong Kong. Thereafter, life became difficult for KAM Lei in Macau and within two weeks HUI reported that TANG had asked him to go to Macau and escort KAM Lei back to Hong Kong.

If KAM Lei returned to Hong Kong then TANG had to ensure that she was looked after as the last thing he wanted was a disgruntled KAM Lei coming to the attention of the police. In pursuance of this objective he made a serious miscalculation – he approached WONG Ying-hung the manager of the Chiu Chow Night-Club in Causeway Bay for assistance. He asked WONG to employ KAM at a good salary as an intermission singer in the night-club and he would reimburse WONG. A cost-free singer was good business as far as WONG was concerned so he agreed and KAM Lei achieved her ambition to become a night-club singer. However, WONG was also from Chiu Chow and he kept LUI Lok informed about the arrangement. When TANG enlisted the aid of WONG in persuading KAM Lei to write a note admitting that she had fabricated the story of being in the car with TANG on the night of the traffic offence Wong agreed, but before showing the note to TANG he took it to LUI Lok who had it photographed.

The police now felt that there was enough evidence to prosecute TANG on charges on perjury and conspiracy to defeat the course of justice. The Legal Department agreed with this opinion and a few days later the Cowboy inveigled his way into accompanying the police officers serving the summonses on TANG.

The case came to trial in the Victoria District Court before His Honour Judge Derek Cons and all went smoothly for the prosecution for the first week and then a bombshell dropped. The constable who was the prime witness in the original trial in the Magistrates' Court recanted his evidence under cross examination and claimed that there had been two similar traffic incidents in mid December the previous year; one involving KAM Lei and her young daughter and the other involving an unknown woman and her young daughter. This version, if true, demolished the case for the prosecution and an application was made to treat the constable as a hostile witness. The application was unsuccessful but the judge suspected there was something 'rotten in the State of Denmark'. He ordered TANG to be held in custody pending the conclusion of the case. Luckily, there was sufficient evidence from other witnesses, particularly KAM Lei, to make a case to answer.

TANG in his evidence claimed that the latest version of events as given by the constable was the truth and that the prosecution was the result of a conspiracy between the police and the Government to silence him for his political activities. On the conclusion of all the evidence from both sides, Judge Cons adjourned the case for two weeks before giving his judgement. The Cowboy was on tenterhooks for the whole period. He had an uneasy feeling that perhaps CID Officers had been 'gilding the lilly' in order to secure a conviction. He made some discreet enquiries and was greatly relieved when he learned from LUI Lok that TANG had approached the constable, using HUI Chi-wing as intermediary, and offered him $20,000 and the guarantee of employment if he changed his evidence sufficiently to raise a doubt in favour of TANG.

Judge Cons reviewed the evidence and found TANG guilty as charged, commenting that TANG was an emotional man incapable of rational thought. Taking into consideration that the case had originated over a trifling traffic case, that the convictions would lead to TANG being struck off the Rolls as a solicitor, that the convictions would inhibit his political ambitions and, finally, that a psychiatric report was before the court, Judge Cons sentenced TANG to be bound over for good behaviour for a period of two years, subject to Tang attending weekly psychiatric counselling sessions.

The constable had resigned from the police force on the conclusion of his evidence by giving a month's salary in lieu of notice but was unable to take up employment in TANG's law office as that was closed. Some ten days later the ex-constable was returning to his tenement cubicle in Western when he was attacked by unknown persons and in falling down the stairs sustained two broken legs and two broken arms. On hearing of the incident the Cowboy wondered if it was just a mere coincidence or it there was any connection with TANG's case. Certainly LUI Lok would not appreciate the loss of face incurred by his being double crossed by one of his own side.

Over the next two days the Cowboy became aware that he was never alone, if some of his own officers were not with him then there always seemed to be a couple of CID officers lurking in the background. He tackled his own sergeant about it and was informed that a directive had come down from CID Headquarters to give him loose coverage to ensure that he did not meet with an accident. He was not sure if this was just the CID covering their own tracks or there was a genuine threat to himself. However, he felt that any such cover was a waste of manpower, an inhibiting influence on his activities and, in any event, unnecessary since he always carried his personal issue revolver. After a couple of days the cover was withdrawn.

TANG appealed against the conviction but the Appeal Court upheld the decision of Judge Cons and he was duly struck off by the Disciplinary Committee of the Law Society.

However, Tang had the last laugh as he then changed his name by Deed of Poll from TANG Hon-tsai to TANG Lut-sze (Solicitor Tang). He then set up in business as an emigration consultant and became quite wealthy.

Chapter Eight

MACAU

Some 450 years ago the first Franciscans Friars and Portuguese seamen landed on the west bank of the estuary of the Pearl River and established one of the earliest, if not the earliest, foreign trading posts on Chinese soil. Over the following centuries the languid little backwater covering a little over six square miles has quietly prospered supporting, but not actively engaged in, trade with China. The land border with China has always been virtually closed and the only access is by sea and this is restricted due to the shallowness of the silted up coastal waters.

Gambling has historically been a major pastime in Macau and in 1934 the Tai Hing Company gained the monopoly to organize all casino-style gambling in the colony and established a series of well-organized casinos catering for Chinese-style games such as Fan Tan and at the same time provided the facilities whereby very attractive young ladies were available to help winning punters to enjoy their newly acquired wealth, thus ensuring that the Company never lost. The reputation of these ladies was such that they almost rivalled the gambling as the main attraction of Macau.

In the aftermath of the war Macau developed into the gold smuggling centre of the world. Gold could be legally imported into Macau and over the following decade an average of twenty million ounces was imported each year which was then smuggled out and sold on the Black Market at vast profit. In 1948 a Cathay Pacific Catalina flying from Hong Kong to Macau, carrying gold bullion and passengers, was the target of the world's first recorded attempted criminal sky-jacking. The attempt failed when one of the sky-jackers shot the pilot and the plane crashed into the shallow waters off Macau. Ironically, the sole survivor was the sky-jacker who had shot the pilot and he was not identified as such until several days after the incident.

In 1962 the Sociedade de Turismo e Diversoes de Macau, more commonly referred to as the STDM or simply the Syndicate, gained the gambling monopoly and expanded the casinos to include most Western-style gambling and the construction of the lavish Hotel Lisboa. The syndicate members who included Stanley Ho, the grand-nephew of Sir Robert Hotung, Henry Fok, Teddy Yip and YIP Hon became very wealthy in the following decades to the extent that they are reputed to be among the richest men in Asia. It is doubtful if any of them know, at any one time, the extent of their wealth to the nearest million dollars.

The Cowboy had never visited the Portuguese Colony of Macau so when a report was received alleging corruption in the Hong Kong Immigration Branch Office in Macau he volunteered to take the case. Accordingly a few days later the Cowboy accompanied by a sergeant took a ferry across the estuary of the Pearl River to the Portuguese enclave.

On arrival the pair booked in to a small hotel and then the Cowboy went sightseeing whilst the sergeant went his own way to look up some old contacts. The streets were quiet, peaceful avenues lined with pavement restaurants which offered excellent fare accompanied with good cheap wine. A quick tour of the sleepy colonial backwater included the obligatory visit to the shell of what was once the largest cathedral in the Far East, which is still an excellent vantage point to view the area.

That evening the Cowboy and the sergeant had a good meal then wandered around exploring the night life which seemed far more vibrant than could have been anticipated during the daytime. Expenses for the visit had been strictly limited so the Cowboy and the sergeant contented themselves initially with just looking and watching but eventually they found themselves on the Macau Palace, a floating casino anchored off the Praya, known to the locals as the 'Chak Suen' (Robbery Boat). Pausing at the Tai Sai (dice) table the Cowboy succumbed to temptation and placed his total stake of $50 on 'big' rather than on an individual number which would pay a better return but with obviously less chance of winning. He watched intently as the female croupier opened the dice cup and displayed three dice showing a winning number of fifteen, which doubled his original stake. When the dice were shaken again he let his bet ride and again the winning total displayed was 'big'. He thought for a moment then he let the bet ride again and once again the winning total displayed was 'big'. Now his stake amounted to $400 which was enough to cover the expenses of a good night out.

The Cowboy was superstitious enough to believe that his Welsh luck ran in threes so he collected his winnings, much to the disgust of the sergeant who urged him to continue his winning streak and make big money. As he walked away from the table arguing with the sergeant, he realized that the female croupier was less than happy with the cheapskate Gwai Lo and the sergeant explained that it was the custom for a winner to give a tip to the croupier before leaving the table. Hastily the Cowboy pulled out $20, which he pushed across to the croupier who was only slightly mollified.

They went down to the lower deck where they were joined by a Mama-san to whom the sergeant had an introduction. Shortly afterwards they were joined by two charming Macanese girls whose features and figures combined the best traits of their mixed Chinese and Portuguese ancestry. Negotiations for the ladies to join them for a late supper and then accompany them back to the hotel were quickly concluded – and at a total price that would not have covered a similar arrangement in Hong Kong for one lady.

Supper was a splendid affair of Portuguese chicken washed down with a mellow Portuguese wine taken at a pavement cafe on the main thoroughfare. The streets were almost deserted of traffic and the colonnaded buildings threw soft shadows across the pavement which gave the whole meal an ambience of colonial splendour.

Later in the hotel room the Cowboy left on the light of the *en suite* bathroom to indirectly illuminate the room and more importantly the smooth olive skin of his companion. As they kissed his hand gently cupped her firm breast and he felt her nipple respond to his touch. He replaced his hand with his lips then his hand slid slowly down over her body to rest between her legs. She tensed momentarily then relaxed and the Cowboy could feel the dampness of her love juices. The sheer eroticism of the occasion was such that the Cowboy was able to function twice in the following hour before they fell asleep in each other's arms still coupled together. The Cowboy awoke suddenly to find the girl's head in his lap and his organ responding to the caresses of her tongue. Moments later she swung her body over his and mounted him. He lay back in growing sexual contentment and wondered why it had taken him six years to take a ferry to Macau.

It was mid morning before the Cowboy made it to the British Consulate which was located in a large colonial-style building set back from the waterfront causeway. Norman Ions, the British Consul, was a mediocre career diplomat now in his late forties who could be considered to have reached the pinnacle of his Foreign Office Service. He greeted the Cowboy with a limp, sweaty handshake and explained the supervision of the Immigration Branch Office was carried out by John Rosen, Vice-Consul, who would not be available until after lunch. The Cowboy happily returned to the hotel to get a couple of hours more sleep.

On his return to the Consulate he met John Rosen a bluff,

cheery Cornishman with whom he established an instant rapport. They discussed the allegation of corruption and quickly decided that it was untrue, as it was not feasible in the system in which the visas were issued. However, Rosen agreed that the Cowboy should stay for at least one or two days to interview the immigration officers and personally observe the system in action. The sergeant was left to his own devices, which he welcomed, whilst Rosen and his wife took the Cowboy out for dinner and a tour of the more respectable night spots in Macau. Much to the Cowboy's regret it was far too late, when the Rosens dropped him off at his hotel, for him to venture out again in the direction of the Macau Palace so he went to bed.

The following day the Cowboy, assisted by the sergeant, interviewed the immigration officers on the basis of a 'prevention of corruption survey' as he saw no point in worrying them about an obviously malicious complaint. That evening he again met the Rosens for dinner but this time was able to manoeuvre an early return to the hotel in order to re-visit the Macau Palace. Luck was not with him. His companion of the previous night was not available so the Cowboy decided to gain some face by declining the company of another girl and returned to the hotel alone. Hopefully, he would be able to go back to Macau again in the near future to take advantage of his strategy.

During the following two months the Cowboy managed to get back to Macau three times, spending the evenings in the company of the Rosens. Each time he brought a new red tie for John Rosen since the latter had a fetish about only wearing a plain red tie. After dinner he would return to his hotel room where he would be joined by his special friend from the Macau Palace. Life was on a roll for the Cowboy and he was becoming so attached to his Macanese lady that he started actively looking for a way for her to join him in Hong Kong.

Fate then intervened in the form of the Cultural Revolution

in China which spilled over into Macau. Chanting masses of Communist supporters took to the streets and the Portuguese authorities seemed powerless to intervene. Ho Yin who was the *de facto* representative of China's interests in Macau seemed unable to influence the mood of the restless Chinese populace many of whom dismissed him as a capitalist Fei Mao (fat cat) who had acquired considerable wealth from his years with the Tai Hing Company. The situation deteriorated daily with everything paralysed and anarchy reigning on the streets with many of the Communist supporters anticipating the end of Portuguese rule and the return of the colony to Chinese Sovereignty. The Portuguese authority appeared to be on the verge of giving up the colony and rumours abounded that the Portuguese vessel, the SS *Timor*, was en route to Macau to evacuate Portuguese nationals.

Overnight, the situation changed and it became clear that the Beijing authorities did not wish to recover the colony at that time and to enforce this stance Chinese gunboats took up position in Macau waters to control movement in and out of Macau. Attention then turned on the British Consulate which was surrounded daily by masses chanting the *Thoughts of Chairman Mao* to support the struggle, which had now been initiated by their compatriots in Hong Kong. In the meantime, the Hong Kong government issued a directive banning any visits to Macau by Government servants which, whilst normal, put paid to the Cowboy's embryonic plans.

The decision was taken to evacuate the wives of the two consulate officers from Macau in the interests of their safety. Murray MacLehose (later Lord MacLehose and Governor of Hong Kong), Foreign Office political adviser to the Hong Kong government, was tasked with arranging the evacuation. He learnt that the Cowboy had been a recent and frequent visitor to the British Consulate and was, therefore, familiar with the location and more importantly a not unfamiliar face to the local staff.

The Cowboy was directed to report to MacLehose's office in Central Government Offices, more often referred to in conversation as the Ivory Tower since its inhabitants were considered to have lost touch with the real world. The Cowboy was somewhat nonplussed at the direction as he barely knew of the existence of the post of political adviser. MacLehose quickly outlined the situation in Macau and proposed that the Cowboy should visit as soon as possible and bring the ladies back in accordance with a plan that was being worked on over there. The Cowboy was a little leery of this proposal but it did not seem to occur to MacLehose that the Cowboy might entertain any reservations about going to Macau at such a time.

The following morning the Cowboy took passage on the first ferry to Macau and at least had the comfort of travelling in style as the vessel was half empty. On arrival he passed through the immigration controls without a problem and walked slowly to the Lisboa Hotel. A leisurely coffee there and then he walked slowly towards the Consulate, a taxi from the ferry pier would have been easier but most of the taxi drivers were members of the Communist Transport Workers Union and he thought it wiser to avoid using a taxi. As he approached the Consulate he could see a crowd of several tens gathered outside the closed iron gates at the entrance but the heat of the midday sun induced a lethargy in them. He walked quietly but positively around the crowd and entered through the unlocked gate without arousing any reaction from the crowd.

On entry he found Ions and Rosen engaged in tearing up and burning files in a previously long unused fireplace in the main waiting room. They received him cordially and after a very welcome long cold drink the Cowboy was briefed on the simple plan to evacuate the ladies. During the night the Cowboy would escort the two ladies out of the Consulate and along the Praya to a waiting sampan which would be crewed by a cousin of a Macanese secretary in the Consulate. The sampan would take them around to the ferry pier and they would then board the first ferry to Hong Kong. It seemed ridiculously easy but the Cowboy had an idea that it would not be that simple. An idea that grew in strength when Rosen took him into his study and produced from behind a pile of ageing file covers an ancient Webley pistol and five rounds which he offered to the Cowboy for protection. The fact that the Webley had obviously not been serviced for a couple of decades and only two of the rounds actually fitted the chamber had nothing to do with the Cowboy's decision not to accept the offer.

It was well after midnight when the two ladies finally decided what they would carry in their small overnight bags and completed their farewells to their spouses. The farewells were somewhat prolonged as both females harboured strong inclinations to remain with their husbands, out of a confused sense of duty and loyalty feeling somewhat guilty about deserting them. On reaching the gate in the rear wall to the courtyard the Cowboy discovered that it was rusted in position and could not be opened without waking the whole neighbourhood. He cursed himself for not having checked earlier during daylight but had not done so to avoid drawing attention to the gate. He now realized why the crowds had never bothered to place a guard on the gate. There was nothing else but for the ladies to climb over the wall and now he regretted directing the two husbands to remain inside.

Mrs Ions gave a little gasp of indignation when the Cowboy helped her up the wall with a firm push on her buttocks and Mrs Rosen avoided the indignity by springing lightly up on to the wall and dropping quietly over the other side. The Cowboy had a theory that attempts at surreptitious movement more often than not attracted the attention it was designed to avoid so the trio walked slowly and positively along the rear alley until well clear of the Consulate and then walked down to the waterfront. Obvious landmarks by daylight were swallowed in the blanket of the night and the gentle breeze rustling through the branches of the trees did little to reassure the trio. Eventually, a voice quietly hailed them from out of the night then there was a splash as the sampan came alongside the Praya. They lowered themselves down into the boat and the Cowboy thanked the gods that at least the tide was high so that for once nature was on their side.

The sampan made slow progress across the harbour with only gentle sculling and the ebbing tide lapped them. At long last they reached the ferry pier and the final obstacle was the wet, slippery iron rung ladder up the side of the pier. Quietly, they made their way to the waiting room and retreated to the respective male and female toilets to await dawn. The Cowboy secured himself in a cubicle and settled down to wait with a well-deserved cigarette only to discover that the packet had been soaked during the sampan ride. The lack of a cigarette seemed to prolong the wait and the Cowboy soon discovered that a toilet seat was not designed for comfort.

At last dawn came and with it the bustle of people as preparations were made for the departure of the first ferry. The trio emerged independently and kept apart from each other until it was time to board which they did using the tickets they had been given on the sampan. The two ladies relaxed and started chatting animatedly as soon as the ferry put to sea but the Cowboy, remembering an old film starring Curt Jurgens in which a ferry was intercepted on the high seas, did not relax until well inside Hong Kong waters with Green Island on the bow.

Chapter Nine

THE RAPIST

In 1967 Communists in Hong Kong apparently believed that the Cultural Revolution which was sweeping China was also the signal for the end of colonial rule in Hong Kong. They were encouraged in this belief by events the previous year in the Portuguese Colony of Macau where Communist inspired and led civil disturbances brought the Portuguese administration to the brink of abandoning Macau. This action was only averted by the direct intervention of the Beijing authorities reinforced with the stationing of Chinese naval vessels off the coast of the Portuguese colony.

In the British colony the problems started with a dispute in a plastic flower factory in Kowloon and soon escalated. The Communist trade unions called for strikes and teachers in the Communist schools organized their pupils into parades through the streets chanting the *Thoughts of Chairman Mao*. As the summer wore on the situation deteriorated and there were violent clashes between the Communist-led unions supporting strikes and Nationalist Kuomintang-led unions which naturally opposed any strikes. The Hong Kong Police Force were caught in the middle as they tried to restore law and order on the streets. Soon the situation developed into a direct confrontation between the Communist-led organization and the police force which led to the army being called upon to provide aid to the civil power.

The greater majority of the local population were far more concerned with their own livilihoods than with politics and when the disturbances interfered with their business they came out in support of the Security Forces and a number of groups handed in petitions calling upon the Government to restore stability and prosperity. Communist agitators planted 'bombs' in the streets to disrupt transport and whilst many of these bombs were hoaxes there were sufficient real ones planted to kill and maim members of the public and a number the security forces. The Hong Kong Police Force is a paramilitary organization and in response to conditions at the time the Force virtually abandoned its normal constabulary role and mobilized into military-style formations in platoons, companies and even battalions. Strangely, the criminal fraternity did not really take advantage of the situation and there was not an escalation in reports of crime, though the drug divans, brothels and gambling stalls did a flourishing business.

In the late summer Tsuen Wan Police Station started to receive reports of females in the Tai Wo Hau and Kwai Chung public housing estates being molested and some being raped. The local CID made enquiries but, as they were required to move in at least squad strength and have a heavily armed Uniformed Branch escort, they made little headway and anyway priority had to be given to combating the Communist inspired violence on the streets.

The historical socio-economic environment of China dictated that the insular agrestic communities were based on their native villages or towns with which they identified themselves in a very close clan-like manner to the extent that a fellow villager was regarded as a sibling even if there were no direct blood relationship. This bond was as close as any to be found in the clans of Scotland. Thus, when the 'sister' of the senior woman police sergeant in Tsuen Wan Police Station was raped the reaction of all the women officers was greater than normal and it was taken as a very serious loss of face. They made their feelings quite clear to the station's CID officers and whilst the latter made renewed efforts they made no headway in identifying the culprits.

After two weeks of no progress the woman sergeant decided to take matters into her own hands and one morning led an posse of her woman officers into the estates to make their own enquiries. It was an entirely unauthorized expedition but the woman sergeant rationalized that the presence of plain clothes women officers would not provoke a Communist reaction and there would be little sympathy even among Communist ranks for anyone who deliberately attacked the unarmed women. Well aware of the Chinese tradition to mind one's own business and avoid any connection with officialdom, the officers concentrated their efforts on teenage girls and schoolchildren. This paid off when a little 7-year-old girl told them of a teenage youth with a tattoo on his right arm and who often wore a green T-shirt with a red dragon design on the front. This description matched that provided by one of the rape victims.

The women officers returned to the station feeling very pleased with their efforts and the sergeant made her way to the office of Inspector CHAN Kwok-hung who was in charge of CID in the station. CHAN listened to the woman sergeant but initially was reluctant to take any immediate action as he felt any magistrate would be most unlikely to issue a search warrant on the basis of the testimony of a 7-year-old girl and in any event, as he knew full well from his own enquiries, there were many youths with tattoos and many youths with similar T-shirts.

It was now approaching 5 pm and he thought about the mahjong session that had been arranged in the Mess for that evening and the ribbing he would get if he excused himself on the grounds of duty. As he hesitated he once again acknowledged to himself that the sergeant was one of the most attractive women in the station and with that he remembered it was rumoured that the Divisional Superintendent had a soft spot for her. In her present frame of mind he could well imagine her marching into the latter's office to demand action and the last thing that he wanted was for the 'Screaming Skull' to descend upon him again within two days of the previous reaming out for lack of results.

He sighed to himself then picked up the telephone to summon some officers from the Taai Fong (main office). Shortly afterwards his two senior CID sergeants known to all for obvious physical reasons as 'The Rock' (after Rock Hudson) and 'The Weasel' (the animal) entered the office. He briefed them on the information available and directed that they were to turn over the flat in which the suspect resided. If the suspect did indeed match the description of the wanted rapist and they found a T-shirt matching the description of that worn by one of the rapists, the suspect was to be brought back to the station wearing that T-shirt. This would tend to substantiate any subsequent claim that he was wearing it at the time and had been detained as he answered the description of a wanted rapist. It was gilding the lily but it would at least avoid involving the 7-year-old girl and complications arising from lack of a search warrant.

The CID party accompanied by a Uniformed Branch escort went to the premises and shortly afterwards returned to the station in the company of a youth with a tattoo on his right arm and wearing a green T-shirt with a red dragon motif on the front. He was taken into the Taai Fong and for the next five hours he resisted, with almost careless insolence, all attempts by CID officers to get him to talk. The attitude and the evasive manner convinced the CID officers that the suspect had been up to no good even if he were not the rapist, though most by now thought it likely he was guilty.

At 11 pm CHAN decided to call a halt and let the suspect cool his heels in the cells whilst the CID officer got a meal in the canteen before the kitchen closed down for the night. As he led the way out of the Taai Fong he found the woman sergeant and several of her constables loitering in the corridor waiting for news.

The sergeant pointed out that it might not be a good idea to take the pressure off the suspect and suggested that he be handed over to the women officers to continue the questioning whilst the CID officers took a meal and compared notes. Doubting that the women officers would be any more successful than his own men, CHAN agreed to the suggestion. The suspect's hands were handcuffed behind his back and he was handed over to the women officers who marched him down the corridor.

CHAN started to follow his colleagues when he suddenly realized that the suspect had not been taken to the women's police office but into the women's toilet. After a momentary pause curiosity got the better of him and he slowly followed the path of the women officers. Gently opening the door, he could barely restrain his laughter at the sight that confronted him.

The suspect was on his knees in front of the toilet bowl with his trousers hanging down by his ankles as the woman sergeant slowly raised his arms behind him forcing his head down into the toilet basin. She nodded to a colleague who then deliberately flushed the toilet, the suspect being kept in position as the toilet slowly refilled and repeated the exercise again and again. Eventually, she allowed the suspect to rise and she asked him if he had anything to tell her. On receiving no meaningful reply, she repeated the previous exercise again and this time when he was allowed to raise his head the suspect made it clear that he had much he wished to tell. As the suspect rose to his feet and was assisted into his trousers the sergeant grinned across the room to CHAN and said, 'Ah Chan, Sir, I think that he has much to tell you now.'

The suspect was escorted back to the Taai Fong where he kept the CID officers busy writing for the next two hours as he recounted in detail the series of assault and rapes in which he had been involved, including full details of his accomplices.

A series of dawn raids by CID officers netted another five suspects including a 15-year-old who was only too happy to comply with the instructions of his outraged parents to tell all he knew about the rapes.

Subsequently all six appeared in court and were sentenced to various terms of detention or imprisonment but the original suspect never mentioned his visit to the women's police toilets, not even to his solicitor. That would have been too big a loss of face, a factor which the woman sergeant had taken into account.

Chapter Ten

TA KWU LING

At the end of 1967 the Cowboy was transferred to the Frontier Division to take command of Ta Kwu Ling Sub-Divisional Police Station which was located within yards of the Sino-Hong Kong Border. Whilst the overt acts of violence which had punctuated the summer months had died away there was still a high degree of tension in the air. A company of Gurkha soldiers was encamped in the station compound under the command of Major Jack Keen and most patrols were conducted as joint military/police operations. At that time the Border Crossing Points at Lo Wu and Man Kam To also came under Ta Kwu Ling and together with the police posts at Nga Yu, Nam Hang, Pak Fu Shan and Kong Shan gave the Cowboy an extensive area of influence.

In 1842 the British acquired Hong Kong Island from the Chinese authorities and in 1860 acquired the Kowloon Peninsula as far north as the present day Boundary Street. Under the terms of the treaties signed at the respective dates the acquisitions were ceded to Britain in perpetuity. Later in the century the British claimed that for the proper defence and protection of their colony it was necessary to extend the Territory of Hong Kong further north on the Mainland and to include the Outlying Islands and surrounding waters. Under the Convention of Peking (Beijing) signed on 9th June 1898 the required extension was approved in the form of a 99-year lease coming into force on 1st July 1898.

The new northern boundary of the Colony of Hong Kong took in the waters of Deep Bay in the east to the estuary of the

Shum Chun (Shenzhen) River, along the high tide mark on the northern bank of the river to its source west of Ta Kwu Ling, through Pak Kung Au (Old Kung's Pass) to the source of the Sandy River, along the river to the coast at Sha Tau Kok and then the waters of the Mirs Bay in the east. In general it was a practical solution to the establishment of the new Border and followed the natural contours of the countryside but it did not anticipate the silting up of the Shenzhen River so that it changed its course, nor did it anticipate the disappearance of the Sandy River except during periods of torrential rain. Thus there are significant differences in the present and original alignment of the Border with the British line retreating several hundred yards in some areas. The parties did not appreciate the social problems that would arise with the division of village lands on either side of the new Border and more acutely the division of the fishing village of Sha Tau Kok down its main street which was renamed Chun Ying Street (China England Street).

Luckily, common sense prevailed at a local level and free access was provided for farmers to cross the Border to farm their fields and fishermen were allowed to land their catches at Lau Fu Shan and Sha Tau Kok without hindrance. This *laissez-faire* attitude is generally unaffected by the state of relations between Beijing and Hong Kong/London and during the Korean conflict many villagers made significant fortunes smuggling embargoed goods into China whilst smuggling gold and artifacts out of China. During the Confrontation of 1967 this cordial relationship broke down and there were a number of violent clashes including a shoot-out at Sha Tau Kok when heavily armed militiamen crossed into Hong Kong and opened fire on a police post killing five police officers and wounding a score more. Gurkha troops supported by the 17/21st Lancers, who reputedly forgot to bring any live ammunition, moved in to clear the area. The Gurkha troops swept through the area just before dusk, no shots were heard and it was reported that no clashes had occurred. However, there was a strong rumour that a number of rough wooden coffins were later recovered from the area in the dead of night and buried on Sandy Ridge Cemetery, which led to speculation that someone had forgotten about the kukris carried by the Gurkhas.

When the Cowboy took up his new post life was slowly returning to normal along the Border, punctuated by the odd verbal confrontation. One day whilst patrolling the Border Road the Cowboy paused by the International Bridge whereupon the Chinese Border Guard unslung his Type 56 assault rifle (Chinese version of the Russian AK 47), cocked it and took aim at the Cowboy. At a range of twenty-five yards there was little the Cowboy could do, yet to retreat would be a loss of face and to remain was foolhardy. It was not a warm day by any means and as he stood there he could feel the sweat running down his back. After a few moments which seemed like hours to the Cowboy the Chinese Border Guard laughed and lowered his weapon. The Cowboy nodded his head in acknowledgement then turned and slowly walked on his way. Later when discussing the incident some of his more insubordinate junior officers suggested that he had not moved for fear such movement would have relaxed his bowels and caused brown stains in his pristine shorts.

On another occasion when on patrol just after dawn the Cowboy spotted an elderly Chinese male and a young girl making a dash across some open ground towards the Border. A Chinese Border Guard appeared from the bushes and opened fire. Initially he fired short bursts just behind the couple then, when they were yards short of the river, he fired a single aimed shot which brought the man to the ground. The girl fell shrieking beside the man and took his head in her arms. The Border Guard accompanied by a colleague approached at a leisurely pace and on reaching the couple hit the girl with their rifle butts until she fell silent on the ground.

The two bodies remained on the ground until mid afternoon when they were collected by some villagers under armed escort.

The following spring the Police Tactical Unit, from which the riot companies were drawn, decided to sort out their stores and this included disposing of a large quantity of out-dated tear smoke. A company went down to the firing range at San Uk Ling and spent the morning firing off the tear smoke shells and then returned to their base with mission accomplished. Unfortunately, there was low cloud cover that day with just a faint breeze and the tear smoke drifted along the valley and eventually engulfed a group of Chinese Hakka females who had come across the Border to tend to their lands.

On their return to China they described what had happened and it was decided that this was a gross persecution of the innocent masses by the imperialist British capitalists who would have to pay for their crimes. The following morning a crowd of several hundred gathered on the Chinese side of the Border and it soon became obvious that trouble was brewing for Lo Wu. The immigration and customs officers withdrew to a safe distance and the Kowloon-Canton railway staff barricaded themselves in their offices. The Cowboy was summoned to the scene as were the Commander of the Police Frontier Division and his military counterpart, a brigadier. Shortly after everyone had assembled, the crowd, now numbering over 1,000, rushed over the railway bridge which spanned the Shenzhen River and surrounded the police post inside which were three constables, one private and eight senior officers.

The crowd demanded punishment for those responsible for the outrage, compensation for those who had been so gravely injured and an abject apology from the Governor with a guarantee of no future recurrence. Negotiations continued throughout that day and the following day by which time the inhabitants of the post had run out of beer, tea and cigarettes and tempers were running high. At last, in the early hours of the morning, approval came through to break up the seige with minimum of force which, ironically, was considered to be tear smoke. At the appointed time a police riot company moved up along the railway tracks and opened up with a volley of tear smoke. At the same time the defenders of the post joined in by lobbing tear smoke grenades.

In the midst of the fray the Gurkha major nudged the Cowboy and indicated a box of grenades on the parapet. They grabbed a couple each and hurled them; on landing, they exploded scattering burning phosphorous over the crowd. The Brigadier shouted an order to cease throwing the phosphorus but, as his voice was muffled, the Major and the Cowboy could not hear what he shouted and more phosphorus grenades exploded among the crowd who now scattered rapidly in the direction of China. Some jumped off the railway bridge into the Shenzhen River for relief but as soon as they started to climb out on the other bank the phosphorus burst into flame. It was all over in a matter of minutes. Luckily no one sought to identify those responsible for throwing the phosphorus grenades and it is doubtful if it was even included in the official report of the incident.

However, the Police Commander decided that the Cowboy should remain at Lo Wu Post for the next few weeks until everything settled down. Each day for the next two weeks a delegation would come across from China led by a very earnest, bespectacled youth clad in a black Mao-style tunic. On reaching the police post the Cowboy was required to appear and whilst he carefully remained behind the perimeter fence the youth would open with a thirty minute dissertation of the Thoughts of Chairman Mao then Notes would be exchanged.

The ground level on either side of the fence was uneven and on the first day the Cowboy was photographed bending forward to take the Note from the other side. The photograph appeared the next day in the Chinese Press with the caption that the 'Capitalist White Skinned Pig bowed to the invincibility of the Thoughts of Chairman Mao'. Thereafter the Cowboy took care to keep his neck and spine erect at all times, even it meant contortions to reach a proffered Note.

During the opening addresses the youth would often pause to chastise the Cowboy for his stance which he claimed was either showing insincerity, insolence or gross arrogance, depending on whether the Cowboy tucked his thumbs into his belt, his hands into his pockets or crossed his arms over his chest. Finally, one day when the youth was in full flow a constable came out and interrupted him. The bespectacled youth was most indignant at this perceived insult to the illustrious Chairman but the constable merely replied that if he was going to chant the Thoughts then he should at least get them right and proceeded to deliver the correct full version of the passage being quoted. There was a stunned silence outside the fence followed by the quick shuffling of a number of little Red Books. The crowd silently returned to China as the constable had been perfectly correct, having been forced to listen to the Thoughts being broadcast across the Border daily for several months.

That afternoon the Army Observation Post on top of Crest Hill reported a gathering of about 10,000 in the main square of Shenzhen Town. Then came a report of a male in dark clothes being paraded around in a white dunce's hat, the odd reflection gave the impression that the man wore spectacles. After about thirty minutes the man was made to kneel in the middle of the square and was dispatched by a single shot to the back of the head. The Cowboy was never able to confirm that the youth was the person executed but the delegations from China ceased immediately and never returned.

Chapter Eleven

SUNG DYNASTY AND LOK MA CHAU

The Sung (Song) dynasty held sway in China from AD 960 to 1279 until it was finally overthrown by the Mongols. The first invasion from the north came in 1227 and the Sung Court fled south to establish a capital in Hangzhou to become the Southern Sung Dynasty, ceding the land north of the Yangtse River in which the short lived Sai Xia Dynasty was established. In 1211, under the leadership of Genghis Khan, the Mongols breached the Great Wall of China and overcame the Sai Xia Empire. Initially, the Sung Emperors followed a policy of appeasement. This did not satisfy the Mongol ambitions and the invasion southwards continued intermittently over the next five decades until the grandson of Genghis Khan, Kublai Khan, completed the conquest of southern China to create the largest country under one rule there has ever been throughout recorded history.

The last Sung Emperor was a young lad who was brought south by faithful followers in retreat from the invading Mongols. Legend has it that the young emperor eventually crossed the Shenzhen River into what is now the Colony of Hong Kong in the vicinity of the small village of Ha Wan. The royal party rode up into the hills nearby where the young emperor dismounted to view the trail they had just followed. That site became known as Lok Ma Chau (Dismount Horse Promontory) and it is now the location of a police station and a famous tourist look-out.

The party approached a local Hakka village, the name of which is lost in the mists of time, though several claim the honour, and sought sustenance. The villagers were very poor and no one household could produce a dish of food suitable for their honoured guest so, with inspired improvisation, the villagers gathered the best titbits of food that each household could provide – pork, chicken, shrimps, mushrooms and various other vegetables – and mixed the lot in a large wooden bowl. They set the bowl before the emperor claiming that it was a traditional Hakka dish for an honoured guest and the emperor and his party set to with relish. Since then in Hakka villages in the New Territories it has become an annual tradition to 'Sik Poon' (eat the large bowl) in the company of close and honoured friends.

The royal party continued southwards and eventually reached the shoreline near what is now Kowloon City and made camp. Messengers brought news that the Mongols were still in pursuit and the royal party were in despair. The prospect of the young emperor becoming a prisoner of the northern barbarians was inconceivable to his faithful retainers. Eventually, one old retainer took the exhausted young emperor in his arms and climbing onto a large rock plunged into the sea; both were washed away and drowned. This part of the legend is commemorated in that the rock from which they allegedly plunged now stands in Sung Wong Toi (Sung King Rock) Park near the present Kai Tak International Airport whilst there is a Sung Wong Toi Road running through Kowloon City. However the Chinese characters for the name are not strictly correct in that the wrong character has been used and the similar sounding Wong (king) has been used instead of the character Wong (emperor).

The police station at Lok Ma Chau was opened in November 1917 and was originally a two-storey building facing towards China with single-storey annexes running south on either side. During the Japanese Occupation there were further additions including sleeping quarters outside the main perimeter. Following the murder of a European police sergeant at Tai O Station by an Indian constable in 1918, a heavy metal grille was installed on the staircase of the main building to secure the officers' quarters from the rest of the station and it remains in position to this day. A further but less honoured recommendation of the enquiry into the death of the police sergeant was that there should be at least two European officers to each remote station.

In July 1970, following a series of confrontations in Police Headquarters with a very senior officer, the Cowboy was banished overnight from the Police Licensing Office to the remote Lok Ma Chau Police Station. This was a posting which the Cowboy appreciated; it gave him an almost independent command out in the remote countryside. Having been born and brought up in the wilds of Wales the Cowboy enjoyed walking in the morning to the sounds of nature stirring and in the evenings sitting on the verandah overlooking the slow moving Shenzhen River and the rolling paddy fields of China. Officers were only allowed to leave the border area for a period of thirty-six hours each week and the rest of the time were required to be *en poste*.

Most of the time the Cowboy was the only European in the station so life could be boring but at least circumstances forced the Cowboy to brush up his Cantonese and he regained his fluency. Serving here also gave him the opportunity to renew his acquaintanceship with the lady who was to become his wife so, although unintentional, the senior officer had done the Cowboy a major favour in arranging the 'punishment' posting.

Lok Ma Chau was a popular tourist look-out and daily hundreds of tourists came to look over the 'Bamboo Curtain' and view the almost deserted paddy fields of China. The air-conditioned tour buses disgorged their loads in the vehicle park at the bottom of the hill and then the tourists laboured up the steep, single-track access road to the police station which also provided access to the look-out. The majority of

100

the tourists seemed to be elderly retired persons from the United States who were determined to enjoy the fruits of a lifetime of labour by seeing the world. Occasionally there was the odd single young female who, if the Cowboy struck lucky, he was able to arrange to meet in town on his next rest day.

There was also a significant number of Japanese among the tour groups, many of whom were apparently not city residents as they soon offended the Cowboy by ignoring the perfectly good public toilets and urinating on the roadside. After a few were invited to enjoy the hospitality of the station, the tour guides swiftly got the message and made a point of ensuring that their groups were clearly informed about the toilet facilities before disembarking from their buses. Occasionally, some of the older Japanese men would appear to be more interested in the police station and the Cowboy wondered if any were former members of the Japanese Imperial Army who had been accommodated in the station during the Occupation. The station was reputed to be haunted by the ghosts of two Japanese who were killed by local Communist guerilla forces whilst on sentry duty outside the main gate to the station.

A few weeks after his arrival at Lok Ma Chau the Cowboy rose at dawn and went on patrol along the Sino-Hong Kong Border from Ha Wan village to Pak Hok Chau Police Post located in the middle of the Mai Po Marshes at the estuary of the Shenzhen River. All was quiet and peaceful in a human sense but that was far from true of nature. Once again the Cowboy made a mental note to buy a book about birds so that he might learn to identify some of the myriad species that inhabited or visited the area.

It was a glorious August morning and the Cowboy felt so at peace with the world that when he reached the post he accepted a cup of thick, brown liquid that purported to be tea, rather than offend the old sergeant by declining the offer. Some day he would have to explain that the boiling water

101

should be poured over the tea leaves and not boiled together for hours. He called up the station to ask for the station Land Rover to pick him up on its way back to the station and at the same time ordered a breakfast of bacon and eggs to be prepared by his amah on his return.

As the Land Rover reached the bottom of the steep access road to the station the Cowboy noticed a couple of tourist buses disgorging a horde of elderly American tourists easily distinguishable by the henna rinses and loud voices.

After the Cowboy had alighted the Land Rover turned around to take out the dispatches whilst the Cowboy entered the station looking forward to a hearty breakfast. He had barely reached the staircase to his quarters when he heard a distant discord and moments later the Station Guard came rushing in calling that there had been a major accident with the Land Rover on the road outside. The Cowboy ran out of the station followed by a small posse in various states of array or rather disarray. On reaching the top of the slope the Cowboy stopped in stunned amazement.

At the bottom of the slope the Land Rover was resting with its front firmly impacted in the bank and the road between it and him was littered with bodies. He walked slowly down the slope, trying to control a mounting sense of panic, whilst he assessed the number of casualties. The Cowboy was a firm believer that enthusiastic but ill-trained first aid did more harm than good so he directed that no one be moved and blankets be brought to cover the injured to give them some sense of attention and reduce the effect of shock.

In all there were twenty-seven persons lying on the road in various states of distress and pain and the young male tour guide was lying in the vehicle park, having fallen over the side of the road and dropped some thirty feet, sustaining severe head injuries. The injured, aside from the guide, were all elderly Americans of both sexes and strangely none had actually been struck by the Land Rover but had all fallen over in attempting to get out of its path.

As he waited for the first of the fleet of ambulances to arrive the Cowboy discovered that one of the group was a doctor and he leapt upon him with relief for professional assistance. The man admitted that he was a doctor but refused to give any form of medical assistance even to identifying the more seriously injured so that they could be accorded priority when the first of the ambulances arrived. The Cowboy, with great restraint, pointed out to the doctor that this was Hong Kong, that he was a police officer who was demanding assistance and that the doctor was required by law to assist. But the doctor was adamant that since the injured were not his patients he would not provide any assistance for fear of civil suits later. At this the Cowboy lost his cool and abruptly told two constables to take the doctor away and stick him in the detention cells.

It took almost two hours for the ambulances to pick up all the injured and remove them first to Fanling Clinic and the more seriously injured on to hospital in town. Then came the problems of arranging for the Land Rover to be recovered and loaded on a truck rather than towed to the police compound for detailed inspection, dealing with the media who had descended upon the scene like jackals at a feast and providing reports to dozens of people, from senior police officers to the Hong Kong Tourist Association, who deemed it necessary to be given a first hand briefing. It was late in the evening when the Cowboy eventually made his way up to his quarters to be confronted by a heaped plate of cold, congealed bacon and eggs.

He sat on the verandah, dressed in his blood-splattered uniform, nursing a stiff drink and wondered just what he had done to annoy the gods. At first he ignored the shrilling of the telephone then the duty officer came up to ask him to take a call from the American Consulate. The caller identified himself as an attache at the Consulate and, after apologizing for the disturbance, explained that he was trying to account for all the tour group and he could not trace a doctor who had been in the group. The Cowboy suddenly remembered with alarm the American doctor still sitting in the detention cells, whom he had forgotten. Quickly he explained to the attache who, to the relief of the Cowboy, was most sympathetic. He thought it would do the doctor good to remain in the cells over night and then, since he wanted to view the scene for his own report, he would come to the station the following morning and pick up the doctor. The Cowboy dashed downstairs to the report room and hastily completed the paper work to cover the arrest and detention of the doctor as a measure of damage control. Keeping clear himself, he arranged for food and blankets for the prisoner then retired for a good night's sleep.

The following morning the attache arrived soon after dawn, took a series of photographs of the site of the accident then joined the Cowboy for breakfast on the verandah – this time the bacon and eggs were hot and fresh. The somewhat chastened doctor was released into the custody of the attache who made it clear that it was only his personal intervention that had saved the doctor from being charged and sent to court. The Cowboy felt that the gods were smiling once more and ordered that a Baai San (Honour to the God Kwan Tai) be held on the next auspicious occasion.

A quiet period followed and the only irritations were the regular inspections of senior officers but usually a couple of days of painting and polishing were sufficient to persuade senior officers that all was well in this generally tranquil oasis.

At the time the Force was engaged in an economy drive and a limitation of 500 miles per vehicle per month was imposed on every police formation. During the annual visit by Mr Rolph, a Deputy Commissioner, the Cowboy pointed out that he only had one vehicle and that each day the vehicle had to go to Frontier Headquarters to deliver and collect dispatches, two or three times a weeks take supplies to the two police border posts and occasionally take prisoners and or case papers to court. These routines journeys were double the imposed limit. Rolph replied that common sense could apply and as long as the journeys were clearly necessary then the Cowboy could, in the circumstances, ignore the limit.

All went well for a few months then came the visit of Mr Slevin the other Deputy Commissioner of Police. It was a disaster from the moment he stepped out of his chauffeured car and noticed a small broken window beside the entrance to the station. The Cowboy explained that it had been damaged during a typhoon some weeks previously and he had repeatedly applied to the Public Works Department for it to be repaired. Slevin just glowered and commented that any officer worth his position would have made repairs within a week. He then espied the station Land Rover, demanded the log books and immediately pounced on the fact that the monthly mileage limit was regularly exceeded.

Again the Cowboy offered his explanation but in doing so overlooked the fact that there was little love lost between Rolph and Slevin. There followed a typical 'Slevinisation' of the station for about two hours by which time the Cowboy was reeling under the weight of a load of minor flaws in his administration. However, that day Slevin was in a reasonable mood and instead of ordering the immediate removal of the Cowboy, as he had done with another officer a week before, he decreed that he would return for a further inspection in two weeks time.

For the next two weeks Lok Ma Chau Station was the scene of feverish activity as every item in the station was cleaned, repaired or polished and any item that was missing or defective was borrowed from sympathetic colleagues at other stations. The Cowboy purchased two dozen clipboards which he hung on the wall beside his desk and filled them with all manner of statistics and returns.

On the fateful day Slevin returned and marched brusquely

into the station. He took a seat in front of the Cowboy's desk. Primed with notes that an aide had prepared for him, he started to cross examine the Cowboy on wide-ranging topics encompassing the number of married men in the station who did not have married quarters, a breakdown of traffic summonses over the past year, number of pupils attending each school in the area and particulars of various village representatives. Each time, the Cowboy reached for a clipboard and read out the required information. This continued for over an hour then Slevin asked how many military patrols had been carried out along the Border and the Cowboy stalled claiming that he could not remember the precise number but that he had the figures and started shuffling a clipboard. Luckily Slevin was satisfied by this time and told him not to bother as the Cowboy, in fact, had no idea or record of the figure. Slevin announced himself satisfied that the Cowboy was now carrying out his duties in a proper manner and with that concluded the inspection.

On one rest day the Cowboy was sitting quietly at the bar in the Dragon Boat Bar of the Hilton Hotel and overheard a couple sitting beside him discussing their recent visit to Lok Ma Chau. When one of them produced photographs purportedly taken inside China, the Cowboy paid more attention and listened to the man explain that he had slipped the police constables a few dollars and they had permitted him to step the other side of the barrier for a photograph. A quick glimpse of the photographs confirmed that they had been taken at the bottom of the road at the barrier to the Frontier Closed Area.

The Cowboy did not disabuse the tourist of his pleasure but on his return to the station he called for the two constables who had been on barrier duty that week. He congratulated them upon their enterprise and initiative and then directed that they were to serve for the next six months at Pak Hok Chau Police Post where they could reflect upon the error of their ways and see if they could find a solution for the mosquito problem that plagued the post. Perhaps not the correct attitude, but it avoided any public scandal which would not have reflected well upon the Cowboy and it served the purpose of discouraging further private enterprise.

In a long tradition originating in feudal history the villages of the New Territories and the Outlying Islands have elected village elders who exercise a form of stewardship over their village. In 1926 the Hong Kong government formally recognized the existence of these village elders with the establishment of the Heung Yee Kuk (Rural Consultative Committee) to act as an advisory body to Government. The system worked well until the late fifties when local rivalries produced such internal dissension that the body no longer functioned effectively.

The Government responded by introducing an Ordinance reconstituting the Heung Yee Kuk as a statutory advisory body with a new constitution. Each village elected their village representatives who in turn elected representatives to a rural committee. There was a total of twenty-seven rural committees and each committee elected a chairman and a vice-chairman who represented the Rural Committee on the Heung Yee Kuk. Unofficial Justices of the Peace were *ex officio* members of the Heung Yee Kuk and they, together with the Rural Committee representatives, elected a further number of special councillors from among prominent personalities in the rural community. It was a limited form of democracy which served the rural area very well and was far in advance of democratic development in the urban areas. The Communist confrontation in 1967 polarized the system and by the end of 1967 some forty-one village representatives had been deregistered as a result of the active participation in what was considered to be Communist subversive activities. It sounded the death knell for the Heung Yee Kuk and over the next two decades the urbanization of the New Territories and the introduction of district boards and a regional council severely eroded the power and influence of the Heung Yee Kuk.

When the Cowboy arrived at Lok Ma Chau the electoral system on the villages was still recovering from the problems of 1967 and many villages were still considered to be Communist enclaves and had to be treated with caution. The clearance of illegal structures in such villages always resulted in major confrontations between the police and the villagers as it was an emotive issue which provided good propaganda opportunities for the Communists. The Cowboy made a point of visiting many of the villages on his own and talking with the villagers and trying to win their support for his role as a police officer.

The first Christmas provided the Cowboy with his own propaganda opportunity by organizing a Christmas party in the station. Over 100 village representatives and prominent personalities in the villages were invited to the station party and the Cowboy took advantage of his links in the entertainment community to lay on what was, by rural standards, a lavish floor show. When the Cowboy explained the problems that he was facing, many of the local entertainers were happy to provide their services free of charge, particularly at a location which overlooked Communist China, whilst the novelty of the location also appealed to a number of the foreign floors shows.

The first Christmas party which started with a Baai San to the Kwan Tai at 10.01 am was an outstanding success with the final stragglers leaving after dusk. Interestingly, a number of the so-called rabid Communists in the area could not resist the temptation to attend and join in the festivities. Needless to say, the following Christmas pressure was put on the Cowboy to arrange another Christmas party and with the generous support of the entertainment community yet another successful function was held. These parties went down in the annals of local history and are still remembered some two decades later.

In September 1970 Dan Grove, the Legal Liaison Officer at the American Consulate General, telephoned to ask if some important visitors could call in at the station for a briefing. In view of the assistance received over the American doctor the Cowboy had no hesitation in extending the hospitality of the station. Accordingly, a couple of mornings later a convoy of long, sleek, black American-manufactured saloon cars laboured up the hill into the compound of the station and disgorged a group of President Nixon's staff which included John Erlichment and George Schultz.

The briefing on China was received with interest but little enthusiasm. Interest rose, however, when the Cowboy mentioned that a decade earlier Richard Nixon had visited the station and had signed the visitors' book. The group did not hesitate to accept an invitation to go up to the verandah to view the book over a small libation. Photographs were taken of the page with Nixon's signature then of various members of the group signing the book. The small libation continued well into the afternoon by which time the drinks cabinet was empty and a happy group departed the station for an evening on the town. Much to the Cowboy's regret he was not able to leave the station and accept the invitation to join them. However, the following morning one of the American saloon cars again laboured up the hill into the compound and the Cowboy was pleasantly surprised to be the recipient of several crates of Canadian Club and Sour Mash.

Chapter Twelve

THE INNOCENT CRUSADER

Mary Evans, the second parlour maid, and James Smith, the footman, had reached what was called an understanding when the Great War that was to end all wars was declared. During the first year events in Europe had little effect upon their lives then the Young Master joined the Army. When he first came back to the house in his officer's uniform it was the cause for celebration but this was short lived as he soon departed for the Front. An innocent sounding term for the morass of trenches where armies of men lived in conditions little better than those enjoyed by sewer rats in the bowels of London, and the cream of European youth died in their thousands. The Young Master was a different person when he came back on leave from the Front and although he did make an effort to join in the parties there was always a strained gaiety to him. James, only a year older, found himself adopting a protective attitude towards his Young Master and took great care to shield him from unwarranted intrusions upon his hours of solitary contemplation.

It was James who answered the door-bell when the postman came with the little buff coloured envelope and it was James who delivered the envelope on a silver platter to the Master as he sat at breakfast. No one in the house was more devastated at the news than James and the war became an increasingly frequent topic of conversation between James and Mary. When Lord Kitchener issued his now famous call for more men to join up, James felt a deep sense of compulsion to volunteer. This was the war to end all wars he reasoned with Mary and, after the war the world would be a better place in which to bring up their children. Mary was not really convinced by these arguments but James was her man and though she feared for his safety she respected his decision.

He joined the Army and after only a few weeks basic training he was ordered to the Front with a batch of other green replacement troops. Mary managed to get two days' holiday and took the train to the port to see James off but the weather in the English Channel was foul and the sailing was postponed for twenty-four hours. James and Mary walked for hours back and forth along the pebbled shore, huddled close to each other thankful for the unexpected bonus of time together. Their emotions ran high so it was, perhaps, only to be expected that lying together in the corner of the breakwater as the dawn approached that nature took its course for the first time in their courtship.

If James had survived that first disastrous attack and returned all would have been different but, three months later as she grieved for her lost love, Mary was comforted by the realization that she was carrying his child. In those days an unmarried mother was a social outcast and considered to be little better than the painted tramps who walked the streets of Piccadilly. When her delicate condition first became apparent the other staff urged her to have an abortion but she refused and later they urged her to put the child into a home but again she refused. The Mistress of the house felt that she had no alternative in the circumstances but to release Mary from service.

Thus, as the Great War finally came to an end and the survivors came back to a country that was supposed to be fit for heroes, Mary was almost destitute and desperately seeking work in order to feed and clothe Ella, her young daughter. She could not return to her small native village below the Brecon Beacons and face her family and friends. As a fallen woman she was sure that in that deeply religious Chapel environment there would be little if any welcome for her and her child. The port of embarkation still held tender memories for her and these drew her back to the pebbled beach once again. As she wandered through the cobbled side streets she came across a small shop with a notice in the window advertising for a housekeeper. She entered and waited quietly until the proprietress was free then enquired about the notice. The elderly proprietress was a friendly soul and noted with a sympathetic eye the strain on Mary's face and the threadbare condition of her clothing so, after giving Mary the particulars of the advertiser, could not refrain from warning Mary that David Phillips was, to say the least, a difficult person and perhaps not all that one could wish for in an employer. Mary thanked her for her concern but explained that now she was desperate for shelter and employment.

David Phillips was, as he was often wont to say, a self-made man and proud of it. Now a bachelor in his early middle age, he had initially been too old to answer the call to war and as the war dragged on he had found it far too profitable to forfeit his then thriving business. A minor ear ailment suffered as a child became a valid medical reason for not joining the Army, and anyway he reasoned his business was helping the war effort. He took a leading role organizing the war effort in the little port and by the time the war ended was a leading citizen with a place on the town council and aspirations to eventually becoming the mayor.

When Mary approached him for the post of housekeeper it was the first time he had ever employed anyone in that capacity so he demanded references and the reasons for leaving her last employer. Mary who was a simple, hard working and very honest person told him her whole story and Phillips was quick to take advantage. A person in his position, he told her, had to be very careful, particularly about employment of domestic staff. Mary could have the post but at a reduced wage as there would be a child in the house. All expenses for the child were to be borne by Mary and in no circumstances was the child to enter the main dwelling part of the house or in any way to disturb him. In order to avoid unnecessary embarrassment he directed that Mary was to say that she was a war widow. Mary had no alternative but to accept these conditions.

The house was quite large as befitted Phillips' new-found station in life and Mary had to work long hours in an effort to keep up with the housekeeping and the demands of Phillips. Success seemed to breed success as far as Phillips was concerned and over the next decade he expanded his business interests and became a major figure in the social structure of the small port town. He was on the board of governors of the new local secondary school and was appointed a Justice of the Peace, sitting each week in the local Magistrates' Court dispensing justice according to the tenets of Phillips.

Despite his financial success Phillips forever complained about the cost of maintaining the household and not infrequently reminded Mary that she only held the post of housekeeper on his good natured sufferance and that he was not responsible for her bastard whelp. Young Ella was horrified with acute embarrassment a few years later when an older girl explained to her the meaning of the term. It was only when she started school that Ella fully realized that her home life was not the same as that of the other children. She had no family except her mother and she suffered pangs of embarrassment when the other children spoke of family gatherings particularly at Christmas time. For a while Ella looked towards Phillips as a father image but these illusions were quickly shattered with his rejection of any contact with her.

A quiet studious child at school who had difficulty in making friends, Ella tended to keep very much to herself. Her home life was equally lonely and the highlight of her day was when Mary came to the bedroom to read passages of the Bible to her before she went to sleep. In the absence of toys or any other books the Bible became the focus of her attention from the time she was able to read and she found much comfort from the teachings of Christ and looked forward eagerly to Sunday School.

When she was 11 she entered the local secondary school and for a few days half hoped that this would win some attention from Phillips who was now the chairman of the board of governors. However, coming home from school early one day, her dreams were shattered when she heard Phillips complaining about the expense of keeping her at school even though schooling by that time was free and Mary paid for her school clothes out of her wages. Ella was barely 17 when her mother died and her rejection was complete as she now had no relations, friends or companions. Phillips reluctantly agreed that she could remain in the house until she completed her schooling but even this concession was conditional on her assuming many of the household duties carried out by her mother.

Ella was a bright girl who worked very hard at her studies and gained admittance to university, together with a small scholarship from the local authorities. She chose to study History and her favourite period was the French Revolution from which the principles of 'Equality-Liberty-Fraternity' had a great appeal. In her second year at university she met William Williams with whom she found she had much in common. Williams was the youngest of a mining family from the Rhondda Valley and his father and six older brothers were all down the pits. A sallow and intense youth, he was very conscious of his working-class origins and resented the affluent life style of his wealthy fellow students with their Oxford bags and roadsters. Initially, it was their mutual interests and common background that drew them together but as they sought refuge in each other's company a deep rooted and idealistic love developed between them. During their last year at university they discovered Marxism which they eagerly adopted as the panacea for the social evils of the world in which they lived.

On graduation they found teaching posts difficult to secure and existed on temporary supplementary positions in various schools whilst Williams became more involved with Communism and eventually joined the Communist Party. When World War II was declared they considered that it was an act of capitalist oppression and Williams was openly vocal in his denunciation of the British government and the war effort. It was not long before some police officers came to their tiny flat and after trashing it in a search for evidence Williams was taken into custody. After a short hearing that Ella considered a travesty, Williams was detained for subversive activities. Within a year he contracted pneumonia and died in the detention camp. The remaining years of war passed for Ella in a haze of bitterness and sorrow.

In 1946 she came across an article in a magazine describing the rebuilding of Hong Kong in the aftermath of the Japanese Occupation and the concept of helping to build a new society held a great appeal for her. She applied and secured the post of teacher at a school in Hong Kong and in early 1947 she arrived full of enthusiasm for her new and meaningful life. She found accommodation considered suitable for an English spinster at the newly renovated Helena May Institute in Garden Road.

Ella was quickly disillusioned to discover that there was little change to the pre-war colonial life style. There was grave injustice and poverty everywhere and in her eyes the Chinese were treated as second-class citizens by their European masters. She felt uncomfortable and embarrassed that there was an amah to clean her room and wash her clothes. She was dismayed to see half-naked Chinese coolies panting in the shafts of rickshaws as they pulled the wealthy upper class around. To her absolute horror she learned that the Hong Kong government still licensed opium divans and actually held public auctions of opium, that odious drug that had tarnished the history of Hong Kong. She wrote long rambling letters of complaint about the continuing opium trade to various departments of the Hong Kong government and later to Members of Parliament and it gave her great satisfaction when a Bill was introduced in the Houses of Parliament to ban opium. She felt that she now had a purpose in life.

She left the protective environment of the Helena May Institute and took up residence in a small cubicle she rented from a Chinese family living in Spring Garden Lane, Wanchai. Her living conditions were spartan and she took her frugal meals with the family. Ablutions at least were conducted in the privacy of her cubicle but the toilet was an insanitary box affair located near the front door and each night black clad females came around carrying buckets suspended from poles over their shoulders to collect the 'night soil'. To Ella this primitive form of sanitation was yet another example of the oppression of the masses and the degradation of the female sex. She plunged herself into a study of the Chinese language and history and soon became a reverse banana. The term 'banana' was coined to describe a Chinese person who has so completely assimilated Western culture that he acts more like a Westerner than a genuine Westerner – yellow (Chinese) on the outside but white (Western) on the inside.

In as far as any generalization about racial characteristics are true the Chinese tend to avoid confrontation and prefer to negotiate through intermediaries. If a Chinese wishes to buy something with which he is not already familiar almost invariably he will first seek out a friend or relative who knows someone in that line of business to provide an introduction. This is particularly true when dealing with government officials since, traditionally, the Chinese have felt that the less contact there is with the Koon (official) the less the potential for problems. Hence when Ella took up residence in a Chinese area and became accepted by them it was not long before neighbours came around seeking her advice, particularly in respect of dealings with officialdom. To Ella the fact that all official dealing, including hearings in the courts, were conducted in English was a gratuitous insult to the Chinese who comprised over ninety per cent of the population. She took delight in taking on government officials on behalf of the poor oppressed masses of Hong Kong, and to her credit often succeeded in her purpose.

During the school holidays she visited Macau where she felt that the Portuguese authorities were less oppressive than the British in Hong Kong. A couple of visits to China filled her with disgust at the rampant corruption and oppression that existed there and she personally welcomed the prospect of a Communist regime coming into power, but at the same time abhorred the fact that it would take war to bring it about.

The early fifties brought a flood of 'political refugees' into Hong Kong from China in the wake of the establishment of a Communist government. Squalid shanty towns flourished on the hillsides of both Hong Kong Island and Kowloon as there was no provision for this human tide. Ella felt considerable compassion for these people, particularly the children, and when she was offered some limited financial assistance in the establishing of a small school on Ma On Shan she had no hesitation in giving up her regular teaching position.

At first she was regarded with a degree of reservation by the population of Ma On Shan since she was the first Gwai Por (devil woman or Westerner) with whom many had ever come into close contact and she was representative of the colonial rulers of Hong Kong. As she walked along the steep narrow paths on the hillside she would be followed by a trail of young children reminiscent of the Pied Piper. Slowly she gained the confidence of the people and became YEE Tai (Madam Yee) based upon her Chinese name YEE Wan-sze (Evans).

117

Although her limited facilities were stretched by the demands of the immediate population it was not long before prospective pupils came from the Shanghaiese enclave that had been established in North Point. These people were generally wealthier than their southern compatriots on Ma On Shan and the children's parents were able to find the financial resources to help her establish a new larger school in the area near the Causeway. She was dedicated to her schools and often worked long hours to meet all the demands placed upon her but she still found time to take up the cudgels on behalf of anyone who she felt was being treated unjustly by the authorities. However, the children were her primary concern and she did not achieve the public recognition of her social work that was accorded to her fellow crusader Elsie Elliot, who was based in Kowloon, though at times she was confused with her.

The Cowboy first clashed with Ella in early 1966 in the course of an investigation into an allegation of corruption in the then Resettlement Department. The complainant claimed to be operating a small but thriving refreshment business in a wooden hut on Ma On Shan. He claimed that the structure was registered as a 'Tolerated Structure' but had been damaged in a typhoon and in the course of repairs the painted registration symbols had been partially erased.

A few weeks previously an officer of the Resettlement Department had come to the structure to check on the status of the structure and after hearing the complainant's story had agreed to check the records in his office. Later, the officer returned and claimed that there was no record of the structure, hence it was an illegal structure which would have to be pulled down. When the complainant protested the officer had offered to amend the records in return for 'tea money' and suggested the sum of $5,000 HK. The complainant had refused to pay and was now in fear that the officer would return and demolish the structure. He did not know the name of the officer but described him as being about 35 years of age, balding and wearing spectacles.

The conversation had taken place within the hearing of a casual customer who was so indignant at the attitude of the official that she had accompanied the complainant to the police station and was willing to support his story. The female customer was also interviewed and supported the story of the complainant.

The Cowboy visited the Resettlement Department and checking through the duty rosters for the area and by a process of elimination identified a suspect who would have been on duty in the Ma On Shan area at the relevant times and matched the given description.

The Cowboy accompanied by a sergeant visited the area with the intention of taking photographs of the structure which could be produced later in court. However, on arrival the Cowboy found that far from being a thriving business, the structure was in a neglected state even for a squatter area, the interior thick with dust and the only sign of a refreshment business was a cobweb-strewn water cooler and some broken chairs.

Whilst the Cowboy took photographs the sergeant made enquiries among the neighbouring huts and discovered that the casual female customer came from the same village in China as the complainant and was a blood cousin of the complainant. More importantly, this particular area was scheduled for clearance in the coming months and during the clearance those occupants of registered structures were entitled to resettlement in one of the new government housing estates, a relatively small sum in compensation and, for those conducting any form of business a ground floor shop in the housing estate. A major windfall for the squatters in that area.

The Cowboy returned to his office and reported his findings to his Superintendent as he was now highly suspicious of the complainant. The Superintendent directed that the enquiries should proceed as there was still a prima-facie case. The sergeant was detailed to carry out surveillance on the complainant as it was obvious that he did not reside in the structure. The Cowboy contacted Chief Inspector CHAN Bing-wing from the then Eastern Police Station to conduct an independent identity parade. On the appointed day he went by prior arrangement to the Resettlement Department and invited the suspect to accompany him back to Eastern Police Station. He also invited eight of the suspect's colleagues to accompany them to participate in the identification parade.

In the potential line the suspect was the only balding person with spectacles so the Cowboy provided all nine persons with identical spectacles and asked them to wear their hats. CHAN was satisfied that the parade was as fair as was practical and asked the Cowboy to leave before the complainant and his witness were called into the room. After about twenty minutes the Cowboy was called back into the room and informed by CHAN that neither of the witnesses had been able to make an identification.

The Resettlement Department officers were thanked for their co-operation and taken back to their office and the complainant was told to come back to the Cowboy's office in a week's time. The complainant, who was followed by the sergeant and some constables, was eventually seen to be living in an apartment building in Oil Street and enquiries established that he had been living there with his family for more than a year. The Cowboy filed his report recommending no further action in respect of the corruption allegation but recommending that the complainant be charged with making a false report and wasting police time. The case file was passed to the Legal Department where Max Lucas agreed with the sentiments expressed by the Cowboy but decreed that the complainant should not be prosecuted as such action might only deter members of the public from making a genuine complaint. When the complainant turned up at the Cowboy's office he was told in no uncertain terms that his allegation was considered to be false and he was lucky not to be facing prosecution. There the matter rested as far as the Cowboy was concerned.

About a month later the Cowboy was summoned to Police Headquarters and informed that a formal complaint of misconduct had been made against him to the Commissioner of Police personally. The Cowboy must have looked stunned as the Senior Superintendent then laughed and reassured him that the complaint had already been checked out, but since it had been lodged by Ella Evans the Commissioner had directed that there must be full compliance with formalities and a statement recorded from the Cowboy and other police officers involved.

The Cowboy was then given sight of the letter from Ella in which she claimed that the complainant was an innocent and honest businessman who had dared to report corruption but had been treated most unjustly by the police officer investigating the complaint. She stated that prior to the identification parade the complainant and his companion had witnessed the corrupt police officer scratching whitewash off the walls of the police station and mixing it with water then smearing it on the faces of those on the identification parade. Naturally under these circumstances, the complainant could not make an honest identification and the guilty person had escaped thanks to the actions of this corrupt officer and she demanded that the officer be dismissed immediately.

After the initial shock had worn off the Cowboy was first amused at the absurd story then indignant and by the time he returned to his office, enraged. He submitted a formal application for approval to sue Ella for libel but this was refused by the Legal Department on the grounds that it was against the public interest. However, the Cowboy gained some indirect compensation the next time he went to the Den in the basement of the Hilton Hotel where he demanded that Max

121

Lucas pay for an evening's drinking and the convivial Max did just that.

There were two young American missionaries teaching at the school and Ella had a good rapport with them. When she had the time, they would have the occasional meal together. The topic of the increasing American involvement in the Vietnam conflict arose in their conversation and all three concurred in their opposition to the American action, which they considered to amount to interference in the internal affairs of another country and a continuation of the French colonial oppression.

Many American servicemen came to Hong Kong on Rest and Recreation visits and when a suitable opportunity arose the two Americans would invite one for dinner and sometimes Ella would be in attendance. On occasion a serviceman would express his disillusionment with the conflict and a reluctance to return to Vietnam. The two Americans sympathized with these sentiments and approached Ella who enlisted the assistance of a Swedish businessman and some Chinese friends. They established a scheme whereby such servicemen could leave Hong Kong and make their way to Sweden and seek refuge there. In all they managed to assist eight servicemen to avoid further service in Vietnam over the following three years.

One day a Chinese friend, TSANG Wai-man approached Ella on behalf of one of her early part-time English lesson students and explained that the student, WONG Kwok-leung, had a problem. WONG had graduated with honours from Hong Kong University where he had been Vice-President of the Students' Union and had now applied for a post as an administrative officer with the Hong Kong government. However, following the Confrontation in 1967 the Government had adopted a policy of not employing anyone who had studied at a Communist school and, unfortunately, the primary school which WONG had attended was a Communist school. Ella remembered WONG as an intelligent and hard working student and had little hesitation about agreeing to the suggestion that she amend the school's old records to show that WONG had studied full time at her school. She thought it rather amusing to put one over on the Government and, if successful, then WONG would be a friend in the enemy camp. In the following years she took a quiet pride at the news of WONG's rapid progress in Government based on his uncanny ability to anticipate and resolve industrial disputes.

The Cowboy had one of his rare free weekends and had spent the Sunday at the Beas River Country Club in the company of Andrene LO, a divorced solicitor, and her 10-year-old Eurasian son. Returning to the urban area Andrene had been in a good mood so she had permitted the Cowboy to drive her Alfa Romeo sports car. Unfortunately, many other urbanites had also spent the day in the New Territories and traffic was heavy returning to town as the dusk fell. As they entered a series of bends near San Wai Bungalows on the Tai Po Road both the Cowboy and Andrene glimpsed a dark shadow to their right, suddenly caught in the headlights of an oncoming goods vehicle, and heard the impact as the vehicle hit the dark mass.

There was a small lay-by ahead of them near the bamboo grove so the Cowboy pulled over and the three of them ran back to see what had happened. Lying in the lights of the now stationary goods vehicle was a man who was apparently unconscious and there was blood trickling from one ear and both nostrils. Lying beside him was a torn paper bag with the shattered remnants of eggs and the Cowboy remembered that the pathway a few yards away led up the hill to a small chicken farm.

Fearing internal injuries, the Cowboy directed that the man not be moved until an ambulance arrived and left Andrene to tend to him whilst he and the lad tried to get traffic moving again to enable the ambulance to reach the scene. An ambulance arrived under the escort of a traffic constable and the injured man was taken away. The driver of the goods vehicle claimed that the injured man had suddenly appeared on the road in front of him and he had been unable to avoid an accident. Andrene and the Cowboy related their fleeting glimpses of the accident. The Cowboy drew attention to the broken eggs and the proximity of the chicken farm, suggesting that the constable confirm the injured man had just obtained the eggs from there.

There the matter rested as far as the Cowboy was concerned but just over three years later it surfaced again. The Cowboy was summoned to Police Headquarters and instructed to go to the recently created Legal Aid Department in connection with a traffic accident and allegations that had been made against him. On arrival the sympathetic duty lawyer showed the Cowboy a letter from Ella Evans in which she demanded justice for the poor injured man. According to the letter two European police officers accompanied by their Chinese floosie had reached the scene of the accident and, ignoring the injured man, had entered into negotiations with the driver of the goods vehicle to blame the accident upon the injured man in return for several thousand dollars.

The Cowboy was astonished at first but recollection of the events came flooding back and he became indignant and then consumed with righteous anger as for once there was sufficient evidence supported by witnesses to show that the allegation was completely false. Once again he applied for permission to sue Ella Evans for libel and when this was refused Andrene sought to take out a private prosecution for libel but the Attorney General of that time intervened and stopped the action. Ella Evans was a popular champion of the masses and as such was a 'sacred cow'. It was, therefore, against the public interest to prosecute her as it could lead to protests and disorder in the streets. Andrene was outraged but the Cowboy in later reflection could never decide what had angered her the most, being accused of corruption or being referred to as a Chinese floosie.

In the passage of time following the aid given to WONG Kwok-leung, Ella developed a deeper friendship with TSANG Wai-man and she enjoyed her stimulating discussions with him since he was a well-educated and urbane person. They seldom disagreed on any subject and she could rely upon him to put everything into perspective and help her to formulate her opinions more clearly.

TSANG, although a refugee from China, was proud of being a Chinese and of the fact that China had a recorded history of culture and civilization reaching back 5,000 years which was far longer than could be claimed by any other civilization or society. He pointed out that a Democrat in America could not help it if a Republican became President nor did an American cease to be an American if he lived outside the United States. Whilst he was critical of some aspects of events in China, such as the Cultural Revolution, he lauded other developments. TSANG felt that under twenty years of Communist government and inspired by Chairman Mao the country had evolved from a backward, feudalistic society where corruption and injustice were prevalent to a stable, industrialized society, a progression that had taken the Western countries several centuries. Within a decade China would become a modern world power and deal on an equal footing with the Western Super Powers.

Ella, reverting to the convictions held in her younger days at university, tended to agree with TSANG. It really came as no surprise to her when TSANG eventually admitted that he functioned as an agent for the Beijing government and used his import/export business as a means of obtaining technical information which was not otherwise available to China. He claimed that although he had joined the Chinese Communist Party in his youth, before coming to Hong Kong he was not a dedicated Communist and was motivated by patriotism. This was something to which Ella found that she could relate without any problem. She saw no harm in using her position as the headmistress of a school on behalf of TSANG, to obtain advanced technical text books and similar publications to which he did not have easy access. On occasion, she followed his counsel on local issues or disputes and exercised her influence as a minor public figure accordingly.

One evening in late 1990 the Cowboy was host to a visitor from the United Kingdom and took him on a tour of the night life of Tsim Sha Tsui. The tour started with a curry in a Pakistani Mess in Chung King Mansion to provide a lining for their stomachs. The first watering-hole was the Red Lips Bar in Lock Street which is one of the oldest and sleaziest bars in the area. None of the waitresses there was under 60 years of age and one old crone, called Josephine, on being bought a 'lady's drink' happily launched into surprisingly clear passages from Shakespeare. Next came a few half price drinks in the Bottom Up served by topless barmaids including Kim, a stunning blonde from Liverpool, and Velvet, a highly articulate Negress from the Bronx. They wandered into the Chin Chin Bar of the Hyatt Hotel but did not stay long as the Cowboy did not feel comfortable in the presence of so many senior Sun Yee On Triad Society office bearers. A few drinks in the In Place Bar in the basement of the Sheraton Hotel and then the Cowboy decided to venture into Tsim Sha Tsui East and visit the hostess clubs.

The Bboss Club had recently changed its name from the Club Volvo when the Volvo Company took exception to the largest hostess club in the world trading under the same name as their prestigious vehicle. The premises were crowded with Japanese tourists and neither the Cowboy nor his companion was sufficiently solvent to compete with their apparently unlimited expense accounts so they did not tarry long.

They wandered out into the night and the Cowboy decided to visit the China City Club. The attendant found them a relatively quiet corner table and after the Mama-san (hostess manageress) found two attractive young English-speaking hostesses to join them they decided to stay around whilst they did some damage to a bottle of Johnny Walker Black Label whisky. In deference to his companion the Cowboy did not disclose that he spoke Cantonese and was amused by the occasional asides in Cantonese between the two girls.

About an hour later a group of four Chinese came and sat at the adjoining table. It was obvious that they had started celebrating very early in the evening and by this time they were feeling very little pain. It was equally obvious that three of them were from Mainland China and the fourth a Hong Kong Chinese who was anxious to impress his guests. Certain hostesses were nominated by the host and he expressed his displeasure in loud, clear terms when he was advised that the hostesses were not immediately available but would join the table after two dance hours (two periods of twelve minutes). The four of them babbled on in Cantonese, which was unusual in the circumstances as Mainland Chinese normally only use Putonghua, the language of China. They cast a few glances at the Cowboy and his companion then dismissed them as Fan Gwailos (foreign devils) who would not be able to understand Cantonese.

The Cowboy paid little conscious attention to their conversation but when his female companion excused herself to visit the 'ladies room' he casually took in more of the conversation and realized with a start that the three visitors from the Mainland were Public Security Bureau officers from Guangzhou and that the local Chinese was also connected to that organization. The Cowboy also excused himself to visit the toilet and took the opportunity on his return to move to a seat closer to the adjoining table. The heavy accents of the alcohol-blurred voices made it difficult to hear the conversation clearly and matters were not assisted by the return of his female companion. However, he realized that the local Chinese was making heavy weather of trying to impress his companions who were somewhat envious of his capitalist life style.

Suddenly the local Chinese stated that there was a 'tung chi' (one of them) in a high position in Government and then came the name WONG Kwok-leung. The name struck a vague bell in the Cowboy's memory and he felt that it was time that he and his companion made a discreet exit. The two young females were not pleased at this move and made it clear that they expected to be given escort (payment made to the establishment for the privilege of taking the females away) and had no objection to accompanying the two back to their hotel to spend the night for suitable renumeration. Rather than draw too much attention to their table the Cowboy agreed to buy them six dance hours each but declined further favours on the ground that he was too tired and had drunk far too much to be able to entertain them.

On leaving, the Cowboy called a halt to the tour and the pair made their way back to the Cowboy's quarters where the Cowboy immediately recorded what he had overheard, on his pocket recorder. He did not trust his alcohol-inflamed brain to be functioning properly the following morning. After several glasses of milk the Cowboy spent a restless night and was away early to the office the next morning. He listened again to his recorder then dictated a report to his secretary. Whilst the report was being typed up he made a few enquiries and confirmed that WONG Kwok-leung was indeed a senior administrative officer with the Government.

The report was passed to another section for further investigations and the Cowboy heard no more about the matter for two months. John Albert Thomas, who was now Director of Special Branch, called the Cowboy into his office and related the outcome of the investigations. Close surveillance of WONG had indeed quickly established that he was an agent of the Guangzhou Branch of the Public

Security Bureau and this had led to a thorough examination of his circumstances.

This examination had uncovered his true education background and the fact that Ella had provided false references for him. Thomas had managed to persuade the Governor that a check had to be made into Ella if only to clear her of any involvement with the Public Security Bureau. This line of enquiry had led to TSANG Wai-man and he, to the surprise of all, was identified as an agent of the Beijing State Security Service. It could not be established, however, if Ella had been a conscious participant in TSANG's activities or an innocent pawn.

The Governor had directed that the results of the investigation were not to become public knowledge for fear of jeopardizing the ongoing negotiations between London and Beijing on the future of Hong Kong. However, the Governor had agreed to TSANG being taken into custody, escorted to the Lo Wu Border Control Point and informally deported. WONG was to be required to resign quietly from Government in the public interest and the Governor was going to interview Ella personally and explain to her that as a result of her activities her continued presence in Hong Kong was not conducive to the future prosperity and stability of Hong Kong.

The Governor must have been very convincing, as befits a professional politician of his stature. Three months later Ella announced to the media that, as a result of increasing health problems, she was giving up her school in Hong Kong and returning to the United Kingdom for treatment. The Cowboy chortled to himself on reading the announcement and the old adage, that he who laughs last laughs loudest, sprang into his mind.

Chapter Thirteen

VIP PROTECTION

In the early 1970s there was a dramatic escalation in acts of international terrorism, particularly by the various Palestinian groups, the German Baader-Meinhoff group, the Italian Red Brigade and in Asia by the Japanese Red Army. In Hong Kong the responsibility at that time for counter-terrorism and the protection of visiting foreign dignitaries was vested in the Special Branch of the Royal Hong Kong Police. The Director of Special Branch, although junior in rank to the Commissioner of Police and, therefore, subordinate to him, was in practice more influential than the Commissioner, having direct access to the Governor of Hong Kong and direct liaison links with the heads of security agencies throughout the Western world.

At this time the Director of Special Branch was Ricky Richardson, a long serving police officer, who had spent nearly all his service in Special Branch. Richardson decided it was time that the Special Branch established a specially trained unit to provide protective security for VIP visitors rather than the current *ad hoc* system of giving the duties to whoever could be made available. It was then the intention to give the command of this new unit to Frank Stewart, a chief inspector, currently serving in Special Branch and Stewart had commenced training for the post. However, during a range course there had been an accident and Stewart had shot himself in the leg whilst practising drawing and firing his Walther PPK semi-automatic pistol. Consequently, Richardson now had to look outside Special Branch for a suitable officer.

In discussion with his senior officers it was decided that the officer given command of the new specialist unit should be physically fit and preferably a bachelor with an aptitude for this type of work.

A few weeks prior to this discussion there had been a demonstration at the entrance to the construction area of the High Island Dam. A group of villagers, exasperated by the problems and inconvenience caused by the work, had armed themselves with poles and erected a barricade on the approach road then detained two Italian site engineers. Special Branch had been aware of the growing feeling of antagonism and the first police officers on the scene had been Willie Worrell the local Special Branch officer and the Cowboy who was in command of the Sai Kung Area. They had surveyed the scene from a safe distance and were aware that a police riot company was en route to the scene.

However, the Cowboy felt that arrival of the company would only escalate the situation since neither side could back away from a violent confrontation without loss of face and anyway it was his patch and therefore his problem. He had handed his gun and cap to Worrell and sauntered down to the milling group with a cigarette in hand. He had sounded off at the villagers in fluent but less than polite colloquial Cantonese and set about dismantling the barricade. The villagers were bemused at the antics of the Chi Sin Gwailo (crazy foreign devil) then saw the humour of the situation. The situation was defused and everyone had gone about their business before the arrival of the police riot company.

As so often happens in life, coincidence was a major factor in Richardson's choice for the post. Only that morning a report on the incident, prepared by Willie Worrell, had reached his desk. Richardson knew of the Cowboy vaguely by reputation and it only took him fifteen minutes and two telephone calls to confirm his impression and arrange for the Cowboy to be transferred to Special Branch the following morning. Such is

131

the power of the Director of Special Branch. The Cowboy was not enamoured at the prospect of a transfer from the role of 'Country Squire' in the rural environment of Sai Kung to the murky offices of the secretive Special Branch and was even less enchanted at being assigned to the Travel Control Section responsible for monitoring movements through the Border Control Points.

It was only several months later when two officers from the Special Air Services arrived to conduct an intensive training course that the Cowboy was informed of the background to his sudden transfer. Coincidence again played a role in that the Cowboy had met one of the officers previously when attending an Explosives Ordnance Disposal Course in the United Kingdom. At the end of a month of intensive training, which emphasized the role of well-trained individuals operating as part of a team, the two SAS officers declared that they were satisfied and the VIP Protection Section of Special Branch officially came into existence.

Richardson decided that a display of the newly acquired skills of the section should be arranged for senior officers in the Force which was a shrewd tactical move as the new section would have to operate in close, open liaison with other police formations. On the appointed day the section went through its drills in a remote area which is now part of the Ocean Park. One long serving senior officer loftily observed to his colleagues that it was all very well in practice but in real life what would happen if the Cowboy were to be incapacitated, as constables could not be expected to act on their own initiative.

The training programme had emphasized not only the need for personnel to act as a team but also the need for initiative and independent action if required. So the Cowboy offered to change roles with a constable of the officer's choice and repeat the drills. The senior officer did not appreciate being put on a spot but he made his choice and further drills were carried out. However, in his anxiety to ensure that nothing went wrong, the Cowboy did not pay attention to his own new role and an error on his part produced a sharp and far from polite rebuke from the constable. It proved the point that all in the section were capable individuals but now the senior officer was not impressed at what he considered to be the insubordination of the constable. The Cowboy realized that in some instances one can never win and made a mental note to be extra careful if he ever had to conduct operations in that officer's area of command.

When the new section was established the Cowboy drew in a few of the personnel who had previous experience in the field but the majority would be newcomers. He was lucky in that the two inspectors serving as the bodyguards to His Excellency The Governor were coming to the end of their tour in Government House and he had no problem in persuading them to join him. They knew each other well and together they made a well balanced team, since David Chan was a dapper, impulsive young officer, who enjoyed the night life of Hong Kong as much as he did gambling, whilst Kit Ng was a more stable mature character who had already settled down in a happy marriage with a beautiful actress. The three of them settled down to select rank and file personnel from the volunteers for the new section.

The Cowboy wanted personnel of strong character who were capable of using their initiative and acting independently as he wanted to create a small cohesive and well balanced team. They culled out the personnel whose records of service comprised a series of bland entries reporting the subjects as steady, reliable, hard working officers, recognizing these entries as platitudes used to describe those who did little and got in to little trouble. Nearly all on the eventual short list had entries praising incidents of good police work which were balanced by adverse comments. It included two constables who had been demoted for insubordination.

The Cowboy won reluctant approval for women officers to be attached to the section on the grounds that a number of their potential charges would be female and who would, on occasion, be in situations where a male escort would be an embarrassment. He also pointed out that in all species the more instinctively and aggressively protective was the female and in this the human female was no different. The approval was perhaps given in a patronizing fashion but nevertheless it was given and Hong Kong became the first to use females as fully integrated members of escort teams. It was a motley crew that came together and from the outset the Cowboy decreed that whilst he was in command and, therefore, responsible for the success or failure of the section, in any operational environment all were expected to contribute and all would be judged upon their performance.

At least twice a week all personnel attended a range course on the indoor range at Police Headquarters and the Cowboy promised to buy lunch for the whole section if on any occasion anyone achieved a higher score than his. Over the following nine years this occurred only twice, although there were numerous close calls.

Range practice concentrated upon close-range instinctive shooting, which is based on the premise that when a person points a finger at an object nature automatically takes over and lines up the finger on the point of focus of the eyes so there is no need to actually aim the finger, a style first introduced by Shanghai Settlement Police some fifty years previously.

The officers spent hours practising until their weapons became an extension of their forefinger then started to fire single rounds. The practice extended to firing two quick shots known as a double tap and then incorporated drawing the weapon from the holster and firing a double tap. In a relatively short time all officers were able to draw and fire three times in ten seconds and score a six-inch grouping at ten yards. The purpose of firing a double tap was to ensure that the potential assailant instantly took no further part in the proceeding as the point of aim was the chest.

Police General Orders required that a police officer should give a verbal warning that he is armed and if the warning is unheeded he may take one deliberate shot aimed at one limb of his target. Quite obviously the training was contrary to these orders and a potential legal hazard if ever the training was put into practice. The Cowboy sought formal approval for the training and some form of cover for any consequences. Eventually, after the Commissioner had personally observed a training session the approval was given in the form of a written authorization from the Commissioner which had to be kept in the Cowboy's safe at all times.

The officers spent hours practising drawing and firing a variety of hand-guns though the general issue was a Walther PPK semi-automatic pistol and .38 Smith & Wesson revolver. The Cowboy managed to acquire a pair of early manufacture Browning Hi Power 9mm pistols from a retiring SAS officer and later a pair of .357 Magnum revolvers which provided the section with a degree of longer range fire power. On principle, however, he tried to avoid the issue of heavy weapons for personnel on close escort duties as he felt this would encourage personnel to engage in a gun fight when the first and overriding objective was to remove the charge from danger as expeditiously as possible.

Traditionally, officers on plain clothes duty in the Force had followed the example of the FBI and carried their weapons, butt to the rear, in waist holsters behind the right hip. Though this style might be suitable when the wearer was in an upright stance on the range, the Cowboy felt it was not the most practical for their type of duty. He pointed out that the gun fights in the film 'Westerns' were just a myth and in fact most of the gunmen of the old West had carried their weapons in a cross-draw position through their belts and generally relied upon shotguns or scatter-guns for gun fights. The officers would spend much of their time working a crowd on their feet, but they would also spend as much time seated, in cars, in restaurants or in hotel corridors and on such occasions a weapon carried butt forwards on the left hip was far more accessible. A further advantage was that a weapon carried in such position was accessible to either hand. Thus, whilst one might instinctively use one's right hand in a defensive gesture, one could always use the left to bring a gun into play.

Although they spent hours on the revolver range the officers spent even more time practising prosaic car drills using one, two or three cars at a time and walking drills, which in the overcrowded environment of Hong Kong were a real headache. Plans were obtained of all the major hotels in Hong Kong and then detailed reconnaissances carried out to the extent that one general manager commented that the officers knew his hotel better than he or any of his staff. Operational commitments only served to interrupt training and over the years the section achieved recognition as a highly professional and well-trained unit. The final accolade for the Cowboy was the sight of a message from Tel Aviv to the security team accompanying General Moshe Dayan on a world tour which instructed the team leader to send the rest of his team ahead to Australia as they were not required in Hong Kong where the local security was first rate.

As part of his general responsibilities the Cowboy became a member of the Government Security Committee and of the Hong Kong International Airport Security Committee and it was in this latter role that the Cowboy experienced his first major problems. Martial Law had been imposed in the Philippines by President Marcos a few years earlier and there was, naturally, some opposition to this move.

One morning the local newspapers carried reports of the safe arrival of some members of the Philippine Opposition in San Francisco which implied that they had escaped there via

Hong Kong. This caused some embarrassment for the Hong Kong government and Cowboy was directed to investigate. For the next four days he and his officers sifted through thousands of Immigration Arrival and Departure Cards in a vain effort to find some trace of the subjects involved. Airline Flight Manifests were also checked but were of little use as the airlines seemed only to be concerned with numbers but not names.

The Cowboy was not looking forward to having to report his complete failure to unearth any trace when a colleague's wife suggested checking the Hong Kong Flying Club which was based on a corner of the airport. Here it was established that a visiting American had hired an aircraft for a day's sea navigational familiarization on the day in question. Further, the aircraft had the capacity to carry five passengers and, if refuelled on the ground in the Philippines, had the range for the distances involved.

All officers were deployed around the airport and eventually a cargo handler and a bus driver were located who had vague memories of a small group of persons walking from the direction of the Flying Club towards the terminal building. It was far from conclusive but it now appeared that the subjects had been flown out of the Philippines on this private aircraft and brought to Hong Kong. On landing, they had casually walked across the hard-standing and entered the terminal building from the air side of the screening channels and up into the departure hall. In the meantime six persons had checked in for the Airline Flight but only one had passed through the Immigration Counters and this one had been carrying the tickets and boarding passes of the other five which he had then handed over to the five subjects.

It was a well conceived scheme and took advantage of many obvious loop holes in the security of the airport. Obviously, access from the air side of the building had to be restricted and this was achieved by sealing most doors from external access whilst an access control system was implemented between the arrivals hall on the ground floor and the departure hall on the first floor.

The Flying Club was requested to exercise greater control and monitoring of all flights particularly those which left Hong Kong airspace. As a general security measure the Cowboy, after consultation with a number of experts, recommended that Airline Check In staff should confirm that the name in a passenger's passport corresponded with the name on the ticket and that the same name appeared on the boarding pass. The Immigration staff should check both the passport and the boarding pass of all departing passengers and, finally, as the passenger boarded, the name on the boarding pass be checked against the Flight Manifest.

The Cowboy was quite pleased with his ideas but the reception soon disillusioned him since the Director of Immigration was most reluctant for any additional responsibility to be imposed upon his staff whilst most of the Airline managers felt the additional work for their staff was most unacceptable and the British Airways Station Manager stated he considered that it would infringe a passenger's right to privacy and, as far as he was concerned, a passenger could use the name Mickey Mouse if he so wished as long as a ticket had been sold. The arguments went on for several months but eventually all the recommendations were implemented.

Generally, protective security coverage was only provided to members of royal families, heads of state, prime ministers and the occasional senior minister who was deemed to be at risk. When the Miss World Beauty Contest was held in Hong Kong a request was made for security coverage and although the Special Branch assessment was that an inherent security risk existed, the responsibility for security was passed to the Uniform Branch – much to the disappointment of the Cowboy. However, the following years more than made up for that disappointment.

The private visit of Earl Mountbatten of Burma in 1974 was a low-key operation. Sergeant Danny Wong was assigned as the close escort and the Cowboy hovered in the background to provide assistance as necessary. All went smoothly until the reception in Beaconsfield House when Keswick, the Taipan of Jardines, accompanied Mountbatten and his aide to the small lift to take the party down to street level. The lift could take only three persons so Wong quickly stepped in front of Keswick and unobtrusively pushed him out of the way. As Keswick watched the lift doors close a squeal of outrage burst from one of his assistants – even the rain seldom dared to fall on the person of the Taipan much less some Chinese manhandle him. The Cowboy saw his career go down in flames before his eyes as he envisaged the complaint that would be on the Commissioner's desk within an hour. He stepped forward and quickly explained that since the lift took only three persons it had been necessary for Wong to push in so that he could accompany Lord Mountbatten out into the street as his bodyguard.

Keswick, as befitted his status, immediately comprehended and reduced his outraged assistant to silence with a look, then apologized profusely for his own unthinking actions asking that his compliments be passed to the officer. On reflection, the Cowboy realized that only one of his team would have dared to do what Wong had done and, perhaps more importantly, that those people, like Keswick, to whom real power and authority come naturally and are secure in themselves are generally far more understanding and approachable than those for whom power is a status symbol.

Some years later Senator Edward Kennedy paid an overnight visit to Hong Kong and at the specific request of the US government protective security was provided for him although he would not normally be so entitled. Kennedy was overweight and scruffy in appearance and throughout the visit treated everyone as if their sole purpose in life was to pamper, him and to cater to his whims. When something in his suite in the Hilton Hotel did not meet with his approval the general manager had to be recalled from his home to personally make amends. Senior consulate staff were sent out on errands that were normally the task of the hotel staff and he was generally selfishly arrogant.

In order to appease Kennedy special facilities were laid on for him at Kai Tak Airport which normally would only be accorded to a head of state and it was arranged that he would not arrive at the airport until the scheduled time for the departure of the commercial Cathay Pacific Flight and would not be inconvenienced by having to wait at the airport or pass through normal passenger channels. This was achieved as a result of considerable diplomatic effort on the part of the Consulate to gain the approval of the various organizations and government departments involved.

On arrival at the airport Kennedy suddenly remembered that he was supposed to contact John Barton, a Hong Kong magistrate, so he demanded that Barton be contacted and brought to the airport. Frantic appeals pointing out that the flight was already fully loaded with passengers and ready for departure and that Barton was then sitting in court hearing a case were to no avail. Eventually Barton was brought to the airport and in breach of all security regulations escorted through to the first class lounge in the departure hall for a ten-minute meeting. The flight eventually got airborne some seventy-five minutes behind schedule and Kennedy departed without any apology for the inconvenience or chaos caused by his whim.

During the late seventies His Excellency El Hadj Omar Bongo, President of the Republic of Gabon paid several visits to the Colony of Hong Kong, each time accompanied by a large entourage and travelling by a privately chartered aircraft. On the first occasion he stayed for four days and was accommodated in the Mandarin Suite of the Mandarin Hotel perhaps one of the most prestigious hotels in the world. There was little known risk to his safety and only one team, under the command of David Chan, was assigned to provide security coverage.

The first night passed without incident but the following day Chan called back to report that there appeared to be some problem with the suite. The Cowboy went around and together with Chan investigated a strange odour that was emanating from the suite. Choosing a time when Bongo was in another suite conferring with his ministers, the Cowboy and Chan entered the plushly furnished suite where the pile on the carpet was high enough to merit a safari guide. In the middle of the room, an aide was squatting before a large silver salver on which he had built a small fire. Around the fire were two ornamental book-ends which held a large silver ice bucket suspended over the fire. As they watched in horror the aide picked a live frog from a container beside him, slit its throat with a knife then dropped it into the ice bucket. Apparently, he was in the process of preparing a snack for Bongo.

The officers withdrew hastily and retreated to their own room from where the Cowboy summoned Peter Stafford the general manager. To his great credit Stafford retained his cool and with great diplomacy suggested that perhaps one of his chefs could assist in the preparation of these special meals. However, the damage was already complete and the foul odour had permeated all the drapes and carpets.

On the second evening President Bongo with his wife and a few aides visited the Captain's Bar in the hotel. The Filipino Trio played some lively dance music and the presidential party were enjoying some relaxing entertainment in the pocket sized dance area when three Shanghaiese couples came into the bar. For some reason one of the males took exception to the exuberance being displayed by the Hak Kwai (Black Devils). The Cowboy hearing the comments took the precaution of asking David CHAN to take to the dance floor with the woman constable. A few minutes later the Shanghaiese group decided that the Hak Kwai could not be allowed to monopolize the dancing and pushed their way onto the floor.

David and his partner tried to keep between the President and the group but eventually were out-flanked by one of the couples who quite deliberately barged into the diminutive President causing him to fall over a chair. David, being Cantonese had little love for any Shanghaiese, retaliated and there was a brief fracas before a quick regrouping and the President was hustled out and back to his suite. Shortly afterwards Peter Stafford was on the telephone to the Cowboy to enquire what had happened as the Shanghaiese party had lodged a complaint with the hotel. The Cowboy explained and once again Stafford was called upon to exercise his diplomacy to resolve the issue.

On the afternoon of the third day Bongo packed his wife off shopping and then left his suite in the company of his Minister of Information, explaining that he was going to hold some private discussions with his staff on another floor and would not leave the hotel. Chan did not interfere but took the precaution of posting one officer to the ground floor lift lobby and one to patrol the floor which Bongo was visiting. About thirty minutes later there was a commotion on the floor which Bongo was visiting and Chan dashed down the rear staircase to that floor.

When peace was restored and Bongo had returned to his suite it was discovered that the Minister of Information had arranged for a private press interview for a female reporter from the *South China Morning Post* and for an assignation with a European prostitute. Bongo had mixed up the two appointments and the female reporter had not been prepared to be groped and thrown on to the bed by Bongo, hence her shrill outcry. Once again Peter Stafford came to the rescue and persuaded the reporter and her editor not to publish any account of the incident in return for complimentary dinners

142

at the Mandarin Grill. Unfortunately, he did not anticipate the *Star* tabloid printing the story with suitable embellishments.

On the final day of the visit the lower ranks of the entourage went ahead to the airport leaving Bongo and his senior entourage to arrive and go directly to the aircraft which was parked on the hard-standing away from the main terminal building. The Cowboy received a frantic call from one of his officers at the airport and on arrival found a scene of complete chaos with boxes and suitcases strewn all around the aircraft. The junior staff had filled the aircraft with the spoils of their shopping forays in Hong Kong and when the more senior staff arrived there was no room for their spoils so physical battles broke out over which items were to be loaded and which were not to be loaded.

In utter amazement the Cowboy watched two senior officers in full dress uniform fighting over the loading of a large television set and when the captain of the aircraft tried to intervene he received a black eye for his pains whilst the television set bounced around on the hard-standing. Eventually, order was restored when the airport authorities agreed to store the surplus freight until arrangements could be made for a charter flight to come and retrieve it. As the aircraft finally taxied off to the runway the Cowboy counted sixty full cargo panniers being towed away for storage.

After Bongo departed the whole floor of the hotel had to be closed off and renovated; it was over a month before the Mandarin Suite could be used again.

On the next visit the management of the Mandarin Hotel declined the honour of accommodating Bongo and his entourage and the lot fell to the Hilton Hotel. The first problem of this visit arose when Philip Mermod, the general manager, telephoned the Cowboy to seek assistance to escort money from the Hong Kong Bank to the hotel. As it was a distance of only fifty yards between the buildings the Cowboy could not see the problem, but when Mermod explained that the sum was two million dollars HK in cash the Cowboy could see the point. Once again Bongo indulged in his favourite treat and once again the best suite in the hotel was placed out of commission as a result of the rank odour of freshly broiled frog.

The following visit the Excelsior Hotel took the chance of accommodating Bongo but this time with a much smaller entourage. The Cowboy liaised with the management in advance of the visit and the whole entourage was accommodated on one floor to enhance security and in standard suites to minimize the potential damage. However, the tariff charged was that of the de luxe suites and the markup on the wine supplied to Bongo's suite should have been enough to cover any damage. On the final visit during the Cowboy's period in office the only hotel which would accept Bongo and his entourage was the Furama, which at that time catered mainly to Japanese tour groups and was most definitely a step down in status.

In May 1976 Mr Zulfikar Ali Bhutto, Prime Minister of the Islamic Republic of Pakistan paid a three-day visit to Hong Kong accompanied by most of his senior ministers and military staff. The private aircraft was parked on the hard-standing away from the main terminal building and as soon as Bhutto came down the ramp the escort team moved in and took him away to the Mandarin Hotel, leaving the rest of the entourage to sort out their own transport with the assistance of consulate staff. On his arriving at the Mandarin there was a small crowd of Pakistanis, mainly police officers, waiting to greet him. Alighting from his vehicle, Bhutto walked up the steps then turned and started to address the assembled crowd. A few minutes later the first of the entourage arrived, among them the Foreign Minister who, seeing a good photo opportunity, pushed quickly through the crowd and started to run up the steps towards Bhutto.

In the escort team was a woman constable known to all as Apple since the Cantonese name for the fruit sounded the same as her name, 'Ping Kwoh'. She glimpsed the Foreign Minister bursting through the crowd and stepping swiftly into his path caught him under the rib cage with her elbow, then as he doubled up she brought her knee hard into his temple sending him flying back down the steps. The rest of the escort team then closed ranks and Bhutto was immediately hustled away to his suite.

Once Bhutto was safely away the Cowboy turned his attention to the fallen man who by this time had been joined by several high ranking Pakistani military officers in full dress uniform. It did not take long to ascertain that the subject of Apple's attention was not a potential assailant. The Cowboy explained to the officers, who included the Commissioner of Police, the circumstances of the most unfortunate incident then followed the entourage into the hotel. The next thirty minutes seemed like a lifetime as the Cowboy waited in the security room and imagined the diplomatic *démarche* that was likely to follow.

Eventually one of Bhutto's aides came out of the suite and politely asked if the Cowboy could spare the Prime Minister a few minutes. This sounded very ominous so the Cowboy prepared to defend himself and Apple for the mistake. To his surprise Bhutto greeted him most warmly and complimented the Cowboy on the serious attitude they had adopted towards his safety and the professional manner in which he and his men approached their work. His military staff had witnessed the incident and were unanimous in their opinion that the Foreign Minister was at fault. Bhutto then insisted that Apple be brought to the suite where he thanked her for her devotion to duty and then required the Foreign Minister to apologize and assure her that he harboured no hard feelings.

On her return to the security room Apple was so embarrassed about the incident that she burst into tears much to the surprise of all present. Up to that moment Apple had never displayed any emotional or physical weakness and had always been ready to take on all comers on even terms, to the extent that all the teams acknowledged her as being a hard case, an image enhanced by her leather outfits and 650cc motorcycle.

The Cowboy thanked the gods that most of the crowd had been police officers so the press did not get wind of the incident and it was noticeable throughout the visit that all the Pakistanis were cautious about coming out of their rooms or making any sudden movements in the presence of Bhutto.

A regular visitor during the seventies was Mrs Imelda Marcos, the wife of President Ferdinand Marcos of the Republic of the Philippines. Although not the head of state, Mrs Marcos was the high profile First Lady of the Philippines and deemed to be at potential risk from supporters of the Moro National Liberation Front and from overseas Filipino dissidents, including Communists, hence coverage was accorded her.

Invariably, a visit by their First Lady provided an excuse for a host of personnel from the various Philippine law enforcement agencies to visit Hong Kong and they usually caused the most problems since they were not declared to the Hong Kong authorities. All too often they managed to bring in or acquire hand-guns, creating the potential for a violent incident between them and the Cowboy's officers.

Luckily, Felix Beiger, the long serving general manager of the Peninsula Hotel, had very good contacts in Manila and was usually the first in Hong Kong to know of an impending visit and he would immediately warn the Cowboy. All Philippine Airline flights from Manila were then made the subject of extra scrutiny. The passenger manifests were checked for familiar names and hotels in Tsim Sha Tsui known to be used by them were checked out. These actions reduced, but never eliminated, the problems. There were usually several armed security personnel travelling with Mrs Marcos and it was always a problem to relieve them of their weapons. On more than one occasion it was done at gun point.

Mrs Marcos was always accompanied by a group of Filipino females known as the Blue Ladies, who seemed to be in constant competition trying to curry favour with the First Lady. In their efforts to outdo each other it was not unknown for some of them to invoke the First Lady's name and claim to be acting upon her instructions. One brought a group of tailors back to the hotel and tried to take them into the secured area, claiming that the First Lady had requested their presence. However, the Cowboy had just taken his leave of Mrs Marcos who had stated her intention of having a couple of hours' rest before the evening's engagements. The Blue Lady was not to be turned away and a confrontation was only avoided by the intercession of the military aide who confirmed that the First Lady was resting.

Mrs Marcos always lived up to her reputation as an inveterate shopper and much of the time was taken up with visits to jewellers but strangely not to any shoe shops. Once she visited a jeweller's shop in the Peninsula Hotel in the company of several of her Blue Ladies. The Cowboy accompanied her, leaving the rest of the team covering the front. The proprietor did not realize that the Cowboy could understand local Cantonese and, on recognizing his customer, he called out to his staff in the rear store to mark up the prices on a number of special items. During the next hour he then produced a number of these items which Mrs Marcos admired and although he was offering 'special discounts', the total value of the potential purchases exceeded $400,000.

The Cowboy took Mrs Marcos to one side and told her what he had overheard, confirming it by removing a newly applied price tag. Mrs Marcos made no comment but merely picked up her handbag and walked out of the shop without making any purchases. The Blue Lady who had taken them to the shop was summoned to the hotel suite, leaving shortly afterwards to take the first available flight back to the Philippines. After that Mrs Marcos came to trust and rely on the Cowboy far more and would often engage him in conversation when travelling by car or walking around the arcades. Although it was sometimes a distraction it also made the role of the Cowboy a little easier as he no longer had to jostle with the Blue Ladies to maintain his position close to his charge.

When the party visited the Trio de Pearl in the then Annexe to the Peninsula Hotel, gaining access was like entering Fort Knox. On hearing the prices being quoted for some of the items the Cowboy acknowledged the justification for heavy security. Mrs Marcos purchased a pair of drop ear-rings of emeralds encrusted with diamonds valued at US $465,000. To the utter amazement of the Cowboy one of the Blue Ladies unzipped an over-night bag and counted out the money in cash. Thereafter the Cowboy detailed an extra officer to join the close cover just to keep an eye on the bag lady.

The ostensible reason for one of her visits was to conclude negotiations for a major contract in the Philippines for which three consortia were contending, including one group who had flown in from London for the meeting. All groups were invited to a dinner party held in the Salisbury Room of the Peninsula Hotel. Mrs Marcos was delayed leaving her suite on the grounds that she was expecting a telephone call from the President and made a grand entrance some ten minutes after everyone else had been seated.

She took her seat at the top table together with her personal friends and guests including Sir Y.K. Pao, then looked around and, addressing the room at large, asked where was her security. Much to the embarrassment, but also amusement, of the Cowboy several tables were moved around. A new table was introduced adjacent to the top table to which the Philippine and Hong Kong security teams shuffled. After taking his seat the Cowboy looked up and caught the eye of Mrs Marcos, who nodded slightly and smiled. Obviously she thought that she was making a point but to whom and for what purpose the Cowboy had no idea.

After the dinner Mrs Marcos moved around and sat for a short period at the table of each consortium before returning to her own table. Various Filipino bands and singers arrived to perform before their First Lady and some people began to dance, including the First Lady. The Cowboy noted that she only danced to lively beat music and never made physical contact with her partner. A Philippine security guard confirmed that she only danced in the arms of the President, which the Cowboy thought was carrying the *grande dame* a little too far. After all, she was only a former beauty queen, not a real queen.

The band changed to a slow tune and as Mrs Marcos left the floor she was intercepted by an Armenian-looking gentleman from the London consortium who attempted to whirl her away. They circled the floor twice then she excused herself and returned to her table whilst her partner returned to his table looking quite pleased with himself. Unfortunately for the consortium, he had not done his homework and that short dance cost the consortium their chance of the contract. Mrs Marcos had great stamina and the party continued into the late hours of the morning until all had left except her own entourage, then she retired.

When working as a close escort the Cowboy would change into a safari suit and sleep on top of the bed so that he could react more quickly in an emergency. On one visit Mrs Marcos retired shortly after midnight so the Cowboy and Andrew LUI, his station sergeant, also retired after checking the night security. LUI undressed down to his underpants and they sat up talking together having a final cigarette and unwinding, then LUI went to the *en suite* bathroom.

The Cowboy heard a stir in the corridor and looked up to

see Mrs Marcos standing in the open doorway. He scrambled to his feet and as she entered he noticed that she had let her hair down so that it fell to her waist. She apologized for any intrusion then sat on the bottom of the bed and grilled the Cowboy in great detail about Hong Kong affairs, developments such as the Cross Harbour Tunnel, tourism, etc. for the next two hours. The Cowboy tried to answer her questions and at the same time was aware of the half naked LUI sheltering in the bathroom and was conscious of movements in the corridor, which he could glimpse in a mirror placed in strategic position for that purpose. He was, honestly, quite relieved when she finally arose and returned to her suite. On checking the bathroom he found that LUI had thrown all the towels and bath mats into the bath and then climbed in and gone to sleep.

The two-day visit of Walter 'Fritz' Mondale, Vice-President of the United States in 1979 was a major operation, though at times it was more like a circus. An advance party of over 100 personnel arrived in Hong Kong three days before Mondale and by the time he arrived the American security detail, including back-up and communication, exceeded 300 personnel. The Cowboy liaised directly with the advance party who, he found, were determined to do things the American way. As always with any American visit there were major battles over the roles and jurisdiction of the respective security teams. The Americans fought to the last second to have some of their personnel carry weapons so that they would be in a position, as they put it, to discharge their responsibility to Congress and to the American people. In the end the Cowboy could not forbear pointing out that their record in this field was worse than that of any 'banana republic'.

The main party travelled out of China by train from Guangzhou and the cowboy and his close escort team boarded the train as it crossed the Sino-Hong Kong Border at Lo Wu. As the train travelled through the New Territories the Cowboy became aware of an army helicopter flying abreast of the train. Unbeknown to him, and despite daily liaison meetings, the Americans had arranged for some of their personnel to link up with an army team to provide cover should an ambush be set up in the paddy fields. The Cowboy reminded them that they were now in Hong Kong – not Viet Nam. He moved back into the VIP coach and since no one made any offer to introduce him to Mondale he sat in a corner to try to get a feel for his charge. He was not overly impressed when Mondale looked up from his note and enquired who was this guy Governor Crawford, referring to Sir Murray Crawford MacLehose. However, he was impressed when he saw Miss Mondale and for a fleeting moment wondering if he could find some excuse to change assignments with George Haring who was to act as her close escort.

On arriving at Kowloon Railway Station the party boarded a fleet of saloon cars and drove to the Hilton Hotel, where the Cowboy found the Americans had arranged directly with the Traffic Police for the traffic flow around the entrance to be reversed for each arrival and departure by Mondale which caused traffic chaos in Central each time. As the motorcade wheeled into the entrance the Cowboy heard Mrs Mondale exclaim that Hong Kong was civilization – she had spotted a MacDonalds.

On the first evening the Mondales were invited to dine at Gaddis in the Peninsula Hotel but Mrs Mondale declined, preferring to send out for a Big Mac and Coca-Cola. Mondale and his group took their seats at the table furthest away from the entrance. This had been previously arranged by the Cowboy who, with another officer, sat at a small table just inside the entrance and the rest of the escort team deployed in the vicinity outside. The Cowboy then realized that there were no secret service personnel in the restaurant and discovered that two had been left outside whilst the rest stood down until the return journey. The Cowboy thought that this was very poor security as the restaurant was a public place and their charge was out of their line of sight. As he knew the *maître d'hôtel* very well it was no problem to arrange for two extra chairs to be provided and he invited the secret servicemen to join him so that they could at least keep an eye on their charge.

On returning to the Hilton Hotel the Cowboy discovered that there had been problems in his absence. The metal detector he had borrowed from the airport and installed in the corridor leading to the secured area had surfaced no less than three secret servicemen still carrying personal hand-guns. The atmosphere was now definitely strained and the Cowboy took delight in adding fuel to the fire by complaining about the escort helicopter which had been arranged without prior reference to himself.

The Cowboy had chosen an extremely reliable and very conscientious sergeant who had a limited command of English, to be responsible for the secure floor of the hotel and had given him clear instructions that no one was to have access to the wing occupied by Mondale if they were not properly identified and escorted by an authorized security officer. Also, all movements were to be logged. The Cowboy knew that the sergeant, called Oddjob for his very close physical resemblance to the character in the James Bond film *Goldfinger*, would not permit anyone to breach the secure area.

Shortly before midnight the Cowboy heard a commotion in the corridor and went to check what was the problem. A middle-aged American dressed in an open necked shirt and braces was looking a little apprehensively at Oddjob who was cuddling a plastic shopping bag in his arms from which protruded the barrel of a Sterling sub-machine-gun. Another American was trying to negotiate with Oddjob with little success. On approaching, the Cowboy discovered that the middle-aged American was the Director of the US Secret Service who had thought to call on Mondale before turning in for the night, the second American was his aide.

No one had identified the Director to Oddjob and he was not carrying any identification, nor had the aide been identified to Oddjob by his predecessor on duty. As far as Oddjob was concerned two unidentified persons were trying to gain access and he was determined that they would not do so. The Cowboy saw the funny side to the situation and luckily so did the Director – at least he did not complain when he mentioned the incident to the Cowboy's own Director over lunch next day.

The following day there was a visit to the Sham Shui Po Vietnamese Refugee Camp which was supposed to be an opportunity for Mondale to gain some insight to the problem but his aides tried to turn it into a photo opportunity. Unfortunately for the aides and the press, the Cowboy was well aware of the potential problems of being swamped by the press if Mondale started shaking hands with the refugees. He had arranged for a crowd control barrier to be erected in front of the refugees and for a press pen to be sited at the end of the barriers. This permitted Mondale unrestricted movement and access to the refugees and also allowed the press a clear view of the proceedings. However, the arrangement did not please the American press who displayed banners protesting about being penned up like pigs, much to the amusement of the secret servicemen who wished that they could get away with a similar arrangement in America without being accused of interfering with the rights of the press.

That afternoon there was a reception hosted by the American Chamber of Commerce at the American Club. Since all present were invited guests who had been vetted by the Consulate the Cowboy stepped back and from a safe distance watched Mondale mingle with the guests. Much to his amusement the secret service deployed five agents in the room with Mondale, which contrasted sharply with their attitude of the previous evening.

The following day the major event was the departure of the Mondales and the Governor and Lady MacLehose came to the hotel to escort them to the airport. The motorcade lined up outside the hotel and at the appointed time all traffic was stopped to provide a clear way to the airport by turning right outside the hotel against the normal flow of traffic and across the junction into Queensway.

Mondale and the Governor got into the first Crown car and, as it moved off, the lead escort car eased into position to lead the way, the close escort car slipping in behind it. The second Crown car with Mrs Mondale, Miss Mondale and Lady MacLehose was supposed to follow the close escort car but the secret service car, with left-hand drive, imported for the visit, moved off prematurely and rammed the Crown car. The motorcade halted for a moment but the Cowboy ordered it to continue as the principal was now in the open and vulnerable. Traffic officers buzzed around like bees after honey and the motorcade linked up on the approach to the Cross Harbour Tunnel which was deserted for the first time in the Cowboy's experience. The rest of the departure ceremony went smoothly and Mondale departed Hong Kong. Sir Murray MacLehose was obviously not very impressed with the visit. On his return to Government House he directed that the account for the cost of the repairs to the Crown car should be sent to the US Consulate.

Early in his campaign for rehabilitation to a position of political influence, President Nixon made a private visit to China and stopped off in Hong Kong on his way there. The liaison officer at the United States Consulate explained that although Nixon had been required to resign his Office to avoid impeachment, he had been the President and Commander in Chief and was still accorded some privileges, as were Generals and Admirals following their retirement, so security coverage was being requested.

In stark contrast to Vice-President Mondale, Nixon arrived

without any entourage other than two secret service officers who seemed embarrassed at their role and kept a very low profile.

Nixon was safely ensconced in the Peninsula Hotel and the Cowboy, who had decided to take the role of close escort for himself, relaxed in an adjoining room. However, the subject did not retire for the night until after 1 am and the Cowboy was somewhat surprised to be alerted at 5 am and informed that the subject was up and moving about. The two secret servicemen were also alerted but did not seem at all surprised. Minutes later Nixon emerged and indicated that he wanted to go for an early morning stroll in the streets so they set off. The Cowboy fell into step beside Nixon to act as guide whilst the remainder of the party tagged along some distance behind.

Walking through Kowloon Park they came across an ancient Chinese man performing his daily 'Tai Chi' exercises and both were quite surprised when the man paused and greeted Nixon warmly in broad American English sympathizing with his loss of Office and claiming to have voted for Nixon in 1960. This put Nixon in a very good humour who, from then on, conversed happily with the Cowboy. He enquired about the possibility of a coffee and roll. The Cowboy led the way to a cafe which was just opening for the morning and the cleaners were still mopping the floor. Nixon bought his coffee with roll and sat at an empty table whilst the two secret servicemen took up position at the far side of the room.

The Cowboy felt a little uncomfortable seeing Nixon sitting in solitary splendour so joined his table, which Nixon seemed to welcome. Eventually it came time to go and Nixon had the bright idea to autograph some of the menus as a form of souvenir for the staff. However, the staff had no idea as to the identity of their patron and started to take exception to the 'Chi Sin Kwai Lo' (Crazy Foreigner) defacing their menus so as the Cowboy escorted Nixon out another officer had to head off the staff and explain the position to them.

It was a little unnerving that a simple gesture could be misinterpreted and could have led to an unpleasant confrontation. Nothing else untoward happened during the two-day visit but it did serve to convince the Cowboy that, despite Watergate, the American public had been well served by their former President.

Henry Kissenger also stayed in Hong Kong on his way into China and the US State Department requested security coverage for him since he still held a high profile political role although out of Office. He was accompanied by a solitary security officer who also acted as an aide. The main event was to be a keynote address at a dinner hosted by Sir Y.K. PAO at the Hilton Hotel which would also be attended by His Excellency the Governor. Protocol demanded that Sir Y.K. PAO should be in position to greet His Excellency, escort him to the reception and immediately return to the foyer to greet Kissenger who was the guest of honour. The press photographers flooded the foyer area and eventually Philip Mermod, the general manager, used his own staff to assist in keeping a clear path for the arriving dignatories. However, the press were not satisfied and wanted more photographs inside the reception to get all three dignatories into one frame and the Cowboy agreed to representations from the public relations officers. Each of the press photographers was required to produce his press credentials to gain entry and no less than six were turned away including one Japanese and one Pakistani for not having any identification.

A bit of a melee broke out in the reception area as the photographers tried to get their exclusive shots and prevent other photographers from getting a good shot, coming to a head when one of their number jostled the Governor who had a hip problem and was not too steady on his feet. The security personnel assisted the public relations officers to ease the photographers out of the area but one persisted in trying to remain behind. A few moments later the Cowboy received

156

a signal to attend the side door entrance on the far side of the room. On arrival he found that one photographer had tried to push his way in and had been intercepted. He recognized the photographer as one with whom he had a problem in the outer foyer and as the one who had been so reluctant to leave the reception area even though free refreshments were being provided for the press in another room. The photographer was firmly ejected and the Cowboy posted Roy Smith to the side entrance to prevent any repetition.

Some twenty minutes later there was a commotion at the side entrance. When the Cowboy investigated he learned that the photographer had made another attempt to gain access and had been forcibly ejected by Roy Smith. This had resulted in a small fracas outside in the foyer as other photographers objected to one of their colleagues being manhandled by police whilst in the course of carrying out his role of witness to the public truth. There was an added problem in that Roy had grabbed the photographer by the seat of his pants and physically pushed him back through the swing doors and the doors had swung back hitting and damaging the camera.

In an effort to defuse the situation the Cowboy called for a Uniform Branch officer from post duty outside the hotel and instructed him to take the photographer back to Central Police Station and there release him with a warning. This resolved the immediate problem but, in the long term, was a major tactical error as the following day the newspaper headlines screamed about the brutal beating of the photographer and Kissenger's keynote address was relegated to inside pages.

Naturally, there followed a formal enquiry which, much to the Cowboy's relief, exonerated the police officers but the subsequent press release only merited a small paragraph tucked away on inside pages. The Cowboy did not escape completely. He received a reprimand for not handling the situation in a professional manner in that he should have charged the photographer with 'obstructing police' rather than letting him go with a warning.

The new Governor of the Portugese Colony of Macau arrived in Hong Kong by air, paid a courtesy visit on the Governor of Hong Kong, then departed for Macau by hydrofoil to take up his post. There was no known security risk and it should have been a routine operation, particularly as it had been made clear that the new Governor would not make any statement until he had arrived in Macau. Unfortunately, when the two governors alighted from the Crown car at Macau Ferry Pier the press representatives surged forward intent upon getting a quick statement. In the ensuing melee the Governor of Hong Kong was unceremoniously pushed over and only the swift reaction of his own bodyguard prevented his fall to the ground. The Governor was not impressed and, at a subsequent meeting at Government House, expressed the view that if the press wished to act like animals then in future they would be treated as such and metal barriers would be erected to pen them in. The Cowboy could not resist an audible chuckle on hearing this authoritative endorsement of his own policy, which had been frequently overruled by the Director of Information Services.

Her Royal Highness Princess Alexandra and her husband, the Honourable Angus Ogilvy, were regular visitors to Hong Kong and in fact had spent part of their honeymoon there. Princess Alexandra approaches her formal duties in a very professional and conscientious manner yet at the same time takes a genuine and caring interest in her work. She is the Honorary Commandant General of the Police Force and always ensures that the Force figures prominently in any programme that is arranged on her behalf. However, as the Cowboy was to learn, she is basically quite shy when in the company of strangers and it is only when she feels comfortable that she relaxes and her sense of humour bubbles forth. In the years that the Cowboy commanded the Protective Security

158

Section the only person to win the respect and admiration of the whole section was Princess Alexandra.

The programme for the first royal visit covered by the Cowboy commenced with a long private weekend at Fanling Lodge, the Governor's holiday home in the New Territories. Prior to the visit the Governor summoned the Cowboy to Government House to brief him on possible venues for private excursions during the weekend. He found that the Cowboy knew the northern New Territories even better than he did and this was the beginning of a good rapport between the Cowboy and the Governor.

After a ceremonial arrival at the airport, Princess Alexandra was escorted by road to Fanling Lodge and naturally every police officer tried to find some excuse to be involved in the exercise. There were constables posted to every road junction, even to dirt tracks along the route. At one stage when the Cowboy looked back the motorcade, which should have comprised only three vehicles, extended to eleven including a police tow-truck. At Fanling Lodge Princess Alexandra had barely entered the building before she dispatched her personal security officer, John Kirchen, to find the Cowboy and express her grave displeasure at the unnecessarily large police deployment, particularly in such inclement weather. It was not an auspicious start to the visit and it was to be a recurring theme throughout all her visits.

The following day the Cowboy took the couple to Mai Po Marshes, which subsequently became a World Wild Life sanctuary, and as they walked along the bunds Angus Ogilvy attempted to make conversation by enquiring about the effect on the Force of the newly established Independent Commission Against Corruption. This was a sensitive topic for most police officers since it was seen by many as a vote of no confidence in the Force. The Cowboy replied that if a similar unit was established in London with the same draconian powers then half the businessmen in the City of London would

159

be in jail. As soon as he spoke the Cowboy regretted it as he remembered that Ogilvy was in the City.

Luckily Angie Law, the woman inspector in the team, struck up a good rapport with Princess Alexandra and over the next few days the damage was repaired. Thereafter a good working relationship flourished between Princess Alexandra and her escort teams and it improved with each visit.

Princess Alexandra tolerated a heavy Uniformed Branch deployment at official functions but she considered it unnecessary for any private excursions and made it clear that she thought the officers could be better deployed on their constabulary duties. She came to accept that it was beyond the overt control of the Cowboy and quite happily entered into minor conspiracies to be smuggled out of Government House to go shopping and would wrap up in a headscarf or duck down behind the seat until clear of Government House. However, unbeknown to her, the Cowboy would tape down the transmit button of his personal radio so that his other escort teams could monitor the conversation and so remain in close proximity at all times.

Currency restrictions were still in force during one visit shortly before Christmas. Princess Alexandra was scrupulous about the fifty pounds limit and the Cowboy gained approval by finding a money-changer who offered a better rate than that offered by the Hong Kong Bank. The team took the princess shopping in Central. Most of the items were too expensive for the budget so a visit to the Chinese Emporium in Queen's Road Central was suggested. As the group walked along they came to a pedestrian crossing and paused at the flashing green pedestrian light, but Her Highness dashed across, jumped for the pavement and then turned and giggled at the ashen faces of the officers who had followed the dash just in front of a CMB bus.

In all she made three visits to the Chinese Emporium and was able to complete all the Christmas shopping without going over budget. It was during these visits that she eventually realized that there were more personnel than just Angie and the Cowboy around as the items purchased disappeared then reappeared at Government House. It is a basic principle of security work that an officer must always have his hands free for his primary role of providing protection even if it means that the subject has to carry some things, so the Cowboy discreetly slipped the items purchased to another member of the team.

Most of the officers smoked, particularly in the boring periods when they were waiting around and Princess Alexandra had an aversion to cigarette smoke. Whenever there was a gap in the official programme which gave rise to the possibility of a private excursion Oddjob, who was always the driver on such occasions, would move the car to a windy spot, open all doors and spray the interior with a deodorant. During one visit the officers discovered that Princess Alexandra was very fond of Toblerone, especially the peppermint or milk chocolate variety that was not available in the United Kingdom Thereafter, each morning when the princess got into the Crown car to depart for a function, there would be a mini bar of Toblerone on the seat.

During one visit there was a function at the Police Sports and Recreation Club for Her Royal Highness to meet officers' wives and families. Someone decided that Mills Barriers used for crowd control should be erected to create a path through the families and that there should be a ring of police cadets around the princess to ensure that no one got too close or jostled her. This created a barrier between her and the people with whom she wanted to meet and talk. As she progressed the Cowboy became aware of her irritation and broke up the ring of police cadets to give her more freedom of movement but a senior officer intervened and the cadets regrouped. Normally Her Highness had a tendency to overrun her programme but that was the only function that she ever left early and although there never was any comment the Cowboy knew that she was far from pleased.

Having returned to Government House early there was now time for a quick shopping excursion. Shortly afterwards the princess was walking in the shopping lanes of Central in the company of Lady MacLehose with an overt escort of John Kirchen, Angie Law and the Cowboy. Kirchen was noticeably hanging back but this did not alert the Cowboy to the potential danger ahead. Suddenly Princess Alexandra turned on the Cowboy and demanded to know if she were at more risk among police families than in the public streets. If not, then why was there such clumsy security imposed on her at the police club. Were she at risk then she had better resign as Commandant General of the Force. The Cowboy tried to explain that it was a mistake probably due to over enthusiasm but this was obviously unacceptable.

Apparently after returning to Government House Lady MacLehose informed the Governor of the scene in the lanes as shortly afterwards the police ADC came out and asked the Cowboy to present himself in the Governor's study as soon as the News was over. The Governor demanded to know, precisely, what had happened to upset Princess Alexandra and the Cowboy had to explain. The programme for the following day was an informal visit to Cheung Chau and Tai O Islands accompanied by the Governor which would also be a photo opportunity for the press. The Governor asked the Cowboy to present his compliments to Roy Henry, Commissioner of Police and David Ford, Director of Information Services and ask them to be in his study in one hour.

The two officers duly arrived and after escorting them to the study the Cowboy turned away but the Governor called him back. The Governor expressed his own and Princess Alexandra's displeasure at the debacle at the police club and his own determination that there would not be a recurrence the following day. The pair of them were to be present and Roy Henry was directed to ensure that the police presence was kept to a minimum and out of sight whilst David Ford was directed to ensure that his personnel controlled the press rabble. To the embarrassment of the Cowboy, the Governor completely ignored the propriety of respective ranks and directed that both officers should take their lead from the Cowboy and that any orders the Cowboy issued would have his authority behind them. He suggested the three of them should immediately review arrangements for the following day. The next hour was extremely difficult for the Cowboy but at least Henry took it as a compliment to the professional ability of one of his men.

The Cowboy had anticipated that the tour of the Islands was going to be a bit of a shambles and the Governor's directives did little to reassure him. If anything went wrong then he was in trouble with the Governor. Even if all went smoothly he was still going to be in a difficult position with Henry and Ford.

As it happened the tour went smoothly with little going wrong. When the party returned to Government House the Governor summoned the Cowboy to enquire if he had had any problems. On returning to the ante-room both Henry and Ford were waiting for him to find out the verdict. Whilst both were content to hear that the Governor was happy the Cowboy could not help feeling a little uneasy about the future.

Generally, there was a good rapport or at least a degree of mutual respect between the officers in the Protective Security Section and visiting security personnel. However, one visiting security officer irritated the Cowboy shortly after arrival by referring to the Chinese officers as 'slant-eyed Chinks' and demanded that all liaison be conducted with the Cowboy personally. During the visit he frequently alluded to the influence he could exercise over his Head of State and implied that he could cause problems for the Cowboy and the latter's officers if he so chose. He requested that a number of items be bought on his behalf and never made any offer of reimbursement. He often boasted of the sexual conquests he had made as a result of his position, the most recent being the only daughter of an American millionaire and the apple of her father's eye whom, he implied, he might marry.

On the final night the Head of State was dining in Government House and retiring early which afforded the entourage an opportunity to sample the night life of Hong Kong. The security officer approached the Cowboy and stated that he wanted to go out for a few drinks and then try a Chinese girl to see if they were physically any different to Caucasian girls. The Cowboy acceded to this very specific request and took the security officer on a quick tour of a few Wanchai bars and then to the Phoenix Apartments in Lee Hysan Avenue. There, the proprietor greeted the Cowboy warmly and offered the choice of several suites including the Japanese Suite which was furnished in the style of a miniature Japanese garden, the Arabian Suite which was furnished in the style of an Arabian sheik's tent with large cushions for bedding and the Space Room which was furnished like the interior of a rocket with the cockpit-like bed which reverberated as though in motion.

The security officer chose the Japanese Suite and after he was safely ensconced with a cold beer the Cowboy opened negotiations with the proprietor who had been checking which ladies were available. The Cowboy agreed that the lady to be called should be young with a good figure and a reputation for being enthusiastic in her work. However, he added a further requirement: the lady should have a social disease. The proprietor was highly reluctant to comply with that request and at first denied that he knew of any such ladies. The Cowboy offered double the normal fee and a commission for both the proprietor and the lady if the transaction was completed and the proprietor agreed.

Shortly afterwards a very attractive but highly embarrassed

young lady arrived at the apartments but was most reluctant to conduct business. Eventually, she agreed and went to the Japanese Suite where the security officer was waiting with growing impatience.

When she came out half an hour later her social conscience was considerably eased since she found her client to be a rough, unfeeling lout. When the officer emerged he complained about the lady's passive attitude and lack of voluptuousness. The Cowboy tried to apologize for the poor service but the security officer merely made more disparaging comments on the Chinese race, which dissolved any guilty feeling the Cowboy was beginning to harbour. At least in those days AIDS had not been identified as a problem.

Chapter Fourteen

THE BANK ROBBERY

Shortly after 3 pm on a Friday afternoon the Cowboy was summoned to the office of the Director of Special Branch where he was informed that he had been promoted to the rank of superintendent and would receive the formal notice with all due ceremony the next week. Following that he would take over command of the newly created VIP Protection Section in which he was currently serving. The news quite naturally was a subject of celebration so, with no more ado, the Cowboy gathered some colleagues and proceeded to the Captain's Bar of the Mandarin Hotel which was, and still is, one of the highest rated hotels in the world.

Shortly before 5 pm on the same afternoon one LI Wai-bun, an early refugee from Vietnam, entered the Po Sang Bank in Shanghai Street, Kowloon. His timing was well chosen in that there were no other customers on the premises and most of the staff were engaged in closing up for the day. He produced a revolver and declared that it was a robbery.

Everything went wrong for LI. One of the staff pressed the alarm bell which was connected to a console in the emergency control room of the nearby Kowloon Police Headquarters, another released the metal grille fronting the bank whilst two other staff slipped out through the side door into the rear alley and made good their escape. LI fired one shot after the fleeing staff members and then two more into the ceiling to bring the remaining eleven members of staff under control. Lady Luck was still against LI. A police emergency unit patrol vehicle was just turning into Shanghai Street when the alarm sounded and by the time LI looked out through the metal grille the police were already deployed in the street outside.

The police commander decided to adopt a 'policy of inactivity' which entailed surrounding the bank with a heavy blanket of police officers and taking no overt action which might in anyway endanger the lives of the eleven hostages. In the meantime LI secured the hostages' hands with wire he found in a waste paper basket and sat down to work out a solution to his problem. The police managed to establish contact with him by telephone and commenced a long drawn out process of negotiations interrupted, initially, by enterprising media reporters seeking exclusive interviews with LI. Eventually, with the co-operation of the telephone company all telephone lines to the bank except one were cut off, the remaining line dedicated to police use.

As the police organized their response to the situation the possibility of having to resort to firearms was recognized. The police marksmen's unit, an informal group of police officers, under the command of a former Special Air Services officer, who were experts with rifles, were called out and deployed at vantage points around the bank. Unfortunately, the two staff members who had escaped were uncertain whether LI was alone or not thus, although he exposed himself as a clear target several times in the initial few hours, they were unable to neutralize him for fear this would result in a massacre by any remaining companion of LI. The possibility of eventually having to storm the bank was also recognized and since the only officers in the Force at that time with specialist close quarters combat training were the newly formed VIP Protection Section belonging to the secretive Special Branch, the approval of the Commissioner of Police was sought for the section to be put on standby.

By 10 pm only the Cowboy and Brian Haigh, the officer from whom he was to take over command, remained in the Captain's Bar and both were far from sober. When the first telephone call from Police Headquarters summoning them back was received they thought it was a practical joke and took no notice but the commanding tone of the Director's voice on the second call sobered them up instantly and they sheepishly presented themselves to his office post-haste. They were briefed on the situation then retired to their office to contact personnel and organize two teams. Brian Haigh, as the senior and the slightly more sober of the two, decided to take the first standby shift whilst the Cowboy went home, took a cold shower, and grabbed a couple of hours' sleep before returning at dawn.

Dawn found a fragile Cowboy nursing a distinct hangover as he returned. His condition was not helped by getting thoroughly soaked in a heavy downpour as he crossed the compound of the Police Headquarters. Brian Haigh briefed him that the impasse continued, the armed robber or robbers holed up in the bank with up to a dozen hostages and negotiations had continued throughout the night.

Haigh left and the Cowboy spread his jacket over an air conditioner in an attempt to dry it then wandered off in search of some coffee before settling down to watch the siege live on television. In the corridor he met Charles Scofield, an Assistant Director, who was possibly not in the best of moods at having been recalled to the office on his Saturday off and would now miss his day at the Yacht Club. The Cowboy was immediately given a dressing down for wandering around half dressed with a holstered gun on display and advised that his cowboy attitude was not in keeping with his recently attained rank nor was it the conduct expected of a Special Branch officer. Finding a sympathetic secretary, the Cowboy got a cup of black coffee and stumbled back to the security of his own office to reflect on the vagaries of human nature.

About 10 am the Cowboy was instructed to take his team to Kowloon Police Headquarters and report to the Commissioner of Police for a briefing. The Commissioner explained that it had been decided to provide LI with the two cars he had demanded and it was anticipated that LI would emerge from the bank with some hostages as protection and attempt to drive off in one of the cars. However, Shanghai Street was very long and there were literally thousands of spectators gathered outside the police cordons at either end of the street. The car would have to slow down to pass through the barriers and the crowd, so the Cowboy was to position his team in the front ranks of the crowd at either end of the street and if the opportunity arose then the robber was to be taken out. The Cowboy raised a questioning eyebrow at this euphemism. The Commissioner retorted that the Cowboy and his men had received expensive specialist training in this field, now was the time for them to earn their money.

The Cowboy went with his team to Shanghai Street. He located the improvised local command post, a small shop commandeered for the purpose, and reported to Paddy Charles who was in command. After clearing his intended role with Charles, he briefed and deployed his teams then took a look around the colonnade-lined street. It reminded him of the set of *High Noon*. The street hummed with tension and the excited gabble of spectators hidden in darkened recesses. Although the siege had now been in progress for over eighteen hours lethargy had yet to creep in. Somehow there was a sense of excited expectancy pervading the air.

He returned to the command post and was casually looking at some architectural plans of the bank when the sound of a shot emanating from there caused all to pause to confirm that their ears were not playing tricks. A further two shots followed, then Superintendent LAU burst into the command post shouting that the robber had opened fire and some of the hostages were escaping through the door in the metal grille. Charles immediately picked up a telephone from the desk, commenting that he had better report developments to Headquarters.

LAU and the Cowboy ran out into the street and the Cowboy continued in the general direction of the bank when he saw a man with hands tied behind his back jumping up and down agitatedly on the pavement. A female, also with bound hands, came out into the street and the pair then turned to take cover behind a pillar on the pavement. The Cowboy, instinctively continuing towards them, paused momentarily wondering which was the actual bank as there was a row of closed metal grilles, then he saw the small open doorway much closer than he had anticipated. On reaching the darkened doorway he paused again with an uncomfortable feeling in his gut and wondered fleetingly just what the hell he was trying to do, but having come this far in full view of colleagues there was no choice but to carry on and see what happened.

It seemed to take an hour for his eyes to become accustomed to the dark interior after the bright sunlight of the street, then he discerned struggling bodies at the far end of the room behind the bank grilles.

Oh, fuck! he thought in panic, where's the bloody hatchway to get behind the counter.

Those useless plans had not shown the actual layout of the bank and it had never occurred to him to make enquiries. He ran along the counter then, miraculously, there was the hatchway and he plunged through it. As he rose on the other side the staff members gave up their unequal struggle and LI grabbed for the gun which was now lying on the floor. Almost instinctively the Cowboy lashed out and hit LI across the forehead with his cocked Walther PPK – in retrospect not the brightest action to take – then rammed the barrel under LI's chin which served the purpose of stopping any further action by LI. More policemen poured into the bank. LI was handcuffed and searched, his only comment was to murmur that he had only arrived in Hong Kong in March that year.

Confusion reigned inside the bank so the Cowboy mindful of the TV cameras outside dragged LI's coat up to hide the

170

bleeding forehead and with other members of his team hustled LI away to the command post where, with somewhat ill concealed relish, he handed LI over to the custody of Charles. He went back out to the street and tried to light a cigarette, but his hand was shaking too much from the sudden and delayed flow of adrenalin. As he basked in his moment of glory a directive was received from the Commissioner of Police for the Special Branch officers to leave the scene as quickly and discreetly as possible and no mention was to be made in any reports or press releases of the Special Branch involvement.

On their return to Police Headquarters the Special Branch officers were invited to the Gazetted Officers' Mess of which the Cowboy was soon to become an official member. There, other officers including the Commissioner, plied them with drinks until well into the afternoon and the excitement had died down enough for them to go home. Once home, the Cowboy flopped out on his bed and slept for twenty-four hours.

Ballistics officers confirmed that the revolver carried by LI was the same one that had been used in an attempted bank robbery earlier in February. The *modus operandi* used on that occasion was similar and LI answered the general description of the culprit though the bank staff were unable to make a positive identification. That attempted robbery had been a tragic fiasco. A patrolling sergeant casually walking up to the bank was shot dead as he approached the door. This to some extent also explained LI's strange comment to the Cowboy.

The Legal Department accepted that there was evidence to suspect that LI was the murderer of the police officer but decided there was insufficient evidence to proceed with any charges. This news brought some brickbats directed at the Cowboy from colleagues who felt that a dead colleague should have been avenged when a justifiable opportunity arose. LI pleaded guilty to charges of attempted robbery and unlawful detention and was sentenced to a total of fifteen years of which he probably would only have to actually serve about ten years.

The Cowboy consoled himself with an article in a Chinese newspaper which had described him as looking like Alain Delon which did his ego no harm at all.

In the end, the real hero of this incident was WONG Chi-cheung, a young staff member of the bank, who whilst lying bound up on the floor saw an opportunity when LI exasperated with the negotiators, put his gun down on the table. WONG kicked the table away causing the gun to fall to the ground then led the other bound hostages to hinder LI's movements until assistance arrived.

Chapter Fifteen

THE ENCOUNTER WITH TERRORISTS

The Cowboy was just leaving his office at the end of the day when he heard the soft burr of his direct line telephone. He paused, considering whether or not to answer, then decided that as it was the direct line it might be a good idea to take the call.

The German manager of the Lufthansa Airline ticketing office was almost incoherent with excitement and on the third time of telling the Cowboy gathered that two Baader-Meinhoff terrorists had just left the ticketing office. He stalled for time by asking the manager to come around to Police Headquarters with any of the staff who had seen the two alleged terrorists and he would meet them at the main entrance. A flicked glance at the wall clock confirmed that it was now well after 5 pm.

'Shit,' he groaned, as he dashed for the door, 'why do these things always arise just outside office hours when there is no senior officer immediately available?'

Halfway down the first flight of stairs he realized that he had not locked his office door and the Special Branch security officer would now be checking that offices were secured at the end of the day, so he abruptly about turned. Naturally in his haste, he dropped his keys but eventually locked his office just as the security officer came sauntering down the corridor.

He took the stairs down to the first floor in bounds almost knocking over one couple who were sedately walking down. He reached the Directorate Office Suite just as Peter Donald, one of the Assistant Directors was leaving and abruptly intercepted him. He quickly briefed Donald about the telephone call and was mildly amused that the information provoked a reaction in Donald similar to his own. It was quickly ascertained that the remaining Special Branch Directorate officers had already left for their homes and would now be fighting their way through the congested traffic, hence none would be available for some time.

Seated behind his large empty desk top, Donald, who was reputed never to have made a wrong decision in his career by the simple expedient of never committing himself to a positive decision, mused almost to himself that apprehending terrorists was really a CID responsibility and not the responsibility of Special Branch and reached out for his telephone. He telephoned the Gazetted Officers' Mess on the sixth floor and was lucky enough to catch both Jim Morris, the Chief Staff Officer of Operations Branch, and Basil Welsh, Deputy Director of CID, and invited them to attend his office urgently.

Shortly afterwards the Lufthansa office manager accompanied by two German staff and two local Chinese staff arrived and were conducted to the office. A 'Wanted Poster' of members of the Baader-Meinhoff group was produced and all five were positive in their identification of one of the males and one of the females. Not only did the two alleged terrorists match the photographs but both spoke with a distinct German accent and the final proof was a telex just received from Lufthansa Head Office in Germany confirming that the numbers of the two tickets produced by the alleged terrorists matched those of tickets that had been stolen in a Baader-Meinhoff robbery in Germany some months earlier.

No one in the room was in any doubt but that two wanted German terrorists were in Hong Kong, but what to do about it was another matter. The Airline staff were thanked profusely for their assistance and were escorted out by the Cowboy.

Donald declared that Special Branch was charged only with the responsibility for gathering intelligence and would appear to have fulfilled this function. It was now up to other formations to make the arrests and, if necessary, appear in court to give evidence.

Morris, the Chief Staff Officer, pointed out that German terrorists had a very violent reputation and only recently in Antwerp had casually killed two uniformed police officers who had merely come to the door on routine enquiries. He, therefore, had some reservations about committing regular officers in a situation which required specially trained officers.

Donald and Morris then looked pointedly at Welsh, the Deputy Director Crime. The latter accepted that it was a CID responsibility but expressed concern for the safety of his men who were not trained in close combat gun-play. At that all three stared at the Cowboy who was now trying to be as inconspicuous as possible in the corner.

Welsh grinned at the Cowboy then turned to Donald and pointed out that the Cowboy had a reputation for prowess with guns and he and his men had been given specialist weapon training for their VIP protection responsibilities.

Donald demurred on the grounds that the specialist weapons training of the Special Branch personnel was still a sensitive subject and their deployment would require high level approval.

Welsh suggested that the Cowboy and some of his specially trained personnel could be unofficial members of any raiding party to provide cover should the raid degenerate into a gun-fight.

Donald mulled over this for a few moments and, realizing it was an opportunity to share in any subsequent glory but without any risk if anything went wrong, acceded to the request, but only for the Cowboy.

The group then broke up with Welsh returning to his office in CID Headquarters to initiate enquiries into the location of the two alleged terrorists who, from their conversation in the Lufthansa ticketing office, were believed to be staying in one of the myriad cheap guest houses in a complex known as

Chung King Mansions in Tsim Sha Tsui.

The Cowboy went back to his office and after some thought drew out two .357 Magnum revolvers which he carefully loaded with semi-jacketed hollow point bullets. He felt that at a time like this he could well afford to ignore any technicalities about the unauthorized use of such ammunition. He reasoned to himself that a dead terrorist would be most unlikely to complain about any infringement of his civil liberties and human rights and certainly would not be able to motivate other terrorists to target Hong Kong for attack to gain his release.

He slipped one Magnum into a spring release holster nestling under his left shoulder while the second went into a belt holster forward of his right hip. His jacket had been specially made by Sam the Tailor who was highly intrigued when he had been asked to tailor the jacket for carriage of a shoulder holster and the trousers with four extra belt loops to hold a belt holster steady. He had recounted his instructions to many of his clients, which only served to enhance the cowboy reputation of his original client.

Following the sage custom of experienced police officers the Cowboy stopped off for a meal on the way to Kowloon Police Headquarters. On arrival at the CID Taai Fong (main office) the Cowboy was greeted with some good natured banter from his CID colleagues but this did not hide the atmosphere of nervous tensions that was growing in the room. In one corner a blackboard was covered with Chinese characters and roman numerals. After a few minutes the Cowboy realized that it was a record of the floors being checked in each of the blocks comprising Chung King Mansion.

There were six blocks each of twenty storeys and on some floors there were several guest houses, so male and female officers in pairs were checking the guest houses systematically under the guise of Narcotics Bureau officers seeking a Negress

176

suspected to be a drug courier. Such checks by Narcotics Bureau officers were far from rare occurrences in Chung King Mansions, thus the story would be accepted by the regular inhabitants and hopefully would not alert the targets if they became aware of the checks. As each guest house was checked out the officers reported back either by radio or by telephone and slowly the blackboard filled up.

Shortly after 11 pm there was a buzz of excitement when confirmation of the location was reported back to the Taai Fong and jokes about the reliability of Special Branch information died a very natural death. The teams were recalled from Chung King Mansion and a new team under the command of Chief Inspector LI Chung-ming known to his colleagues as Hak Kwai (Black Devil) was dispatched to carry out a detailed reconnaissance of the target guest house. Two hours later Chief Inspector LI returned, leaving his team camped on a rear landing where, with the aid of a mirror, they could see into the lobby area of the guest house. LI reported a sighting of the two suspects seated in the lobby area engaged in conversation with another European male and an Indian male whilst an elderly Chinese male was seated behind a desk near the entrance, apparently the room attendant. The guest house was a small sleazy establishment with about a dozen small rooms, or more precisely cubicles, constructed out of hardboard walling which left much to be desired in terms of habitable accommodation.

Asked for an opinion, the Cowboy advocated a quick rush by two or three armed officers into the lobby and taking the suspects there but as this was being debated the reconnaissance team reported the party breaking up and going into various cubicles. Direction of this operation had been delegated to John Albert Thomas, a relatively young but shrewd and very experienced CID officer hailing originally from Liverpool who, in honour of his birthplace, sported a mild Beatles hair style, though the more cynical of his colleagues claimed he was merely trying to disguise his receding hairline. Thomas decided that in view of the narrow congested layout of the guest house initially only six officers would enter the premises. The Cowboy and LI would hit the suspects' cubicle, the two pairs would take the cubicles of the other European and Indian males. As all of them had only just entered their cubicles he further decided to hold off the raid until 5 am when hopefully all would be fully asleep and advantage would rest with the raiding party.

The next four hours passed very slowly in the Taai Fong, humour when it surfaced seemed forced and was often far more crude than normal. Some officers tried to pass the time playing cards or the more traditional mahjong but the tension rose as did tempers. It was almost a relief when Scouse Thomas came back to the Taai Fong to advise that the Commissioner had been briefed and had in turn briefed the Secretary for Security who had taken it upon himself to disturb His Excellency the Governor and that the latter had sent his best wishes to the officers.

Christ! thought the Cowboy, who normally tried to avoid briefing senior officers in advance, this has all the makings of a ginormous fuck-up. If anything goes down it will be on the front page of the *South China Morning Post* before there is a chance to carry out any damage control.

The motorcade of CID cars proceeded out of Kowloon Headquarters along Prince Edward Road into Nathan Road where a fire tender and some police emergency units were waiting to provide a back up if necessary. The whole motorcade travelled slowly down Nathan Road drawing voluble comments from the early morning crowds and eventually came to a halt in Nathan Road outside the Miramar Hotel. The reconnaissance team reported that all was quiet in the target premises and the raiding party donned their heavy bullet-proof vests and set off down the road accompanied by Thomas and his back up teams.

On arriving at the target block via the rear alleys the Cowboy was bathed in sweat – and he stank to high heaven having failed to notice a large turd on the ground. He decided to discard the heavy bullet-proof vest in order to provide some degree of mobility. In any event he had reservations about being able to use his revolver efficiently whilst encased in the cumbersome vest which chafed his armpits and restricted arm movement.

The party took some time to reach the floor below the target guest house; just one lift was working and that only took three persons at a time. Finally, all was ready and Thomas gave the go ahead to the raiding party. The Cowboy led the way up the last flight of stairs thinking with wry amusement that somehow, as an unofficial presence, he was in the wrong place, then cursed quietly as LI accidentally goosed him with the barrel of an AR15.

The main entrance door was not locked and the dozing room attendant woke up looking into the foreboding visage of Hak Kwai LI, which was enough to deter him from sleeping on duty ever again. The attendant was hustled off the premises whilst the Cowboy and LI checked a vacant cubicle and confirmed that the locks were very flimsy affairs. The other two pairs took up position outside their target cubicles. After giving a thumbs up in the direction of the unseen mirror the Cowboy and LI inched their way down the narrow corridor to their target cubicle.

Problem number one immediately arose: LI found that because of the bullet-proof vest he could only move sideways in the narrow corridor; problem number two was that due to the narrow width it was impossible for him to bring his rifle to bear if he wanted to. LI discarded the rifle and the Cowboy gave him the second Magnum to use and they took up position outside the door. LI crouched slightly to one side whilst the Cowboy braced himself against the opposite wall and raised one booted heel to the level of the door lock. There was a pause as they both looked at each other, shrugged and then the Cowboy kicked the door in.

The double bed was just inside the door and as the figure on the right started to rise the Cowboy poked his Magnum into the figure's face and suggested in no uncertain terms that the person make no further movement. Simultaneously LI had done the same manoeuvre with the figure on the right of the bed. There was complete silence in the room as LI reached over and flicked on the light switch. The tousled couple in the bed were in a state of shock for a moment then the male demanded to know what was going on, in a clear New Zealand accent.

Christ! thought the Cowboy, the shit is beginning to hit the fan already and he could hear a muffled commotion from the other cubicles which was quickly followed by the sound of the back up party entering the premises. LI, following the briefing, hustled the naked male out of the room leaving the Cowboy to look after the woman. Deciding to stick with the original plan for the time being, the Cowboy identified himself and asked for the woman's identity. Moving very slowly with the bed sheet drawn up to her chin the woman pointed to her handbag on the bedside table and when the Cowboy gestured, she reached over for it and in doing so raised the sheet which disclosed a widening wet yellow patch under her naked backside. The passport produced from the handbag seemed genuine and identified the holder as a schoolteacher from New Zealand. The Cowboy decided that it was time he became an unofficial member of the raiding party very rapidly and called for some women police officers to take over.

During the next half-hour it was ascertained that the suspects were teachers from New Zealand who were back-packing through Asia and had purchased the two airline tickets in question for half their face value in a side street in Bangkok. The other European male was a Frenchman who spoke very fractured English but sufficiently to establish that he had no connection with the two teachers. The poor Indian male had been sitting up in his room reading a book and on hearing the initial commotion had turned towards the door, which at that moment had burst inward catching him in the face. Thereafter he had great difficulty in stanching the flow of blood from his nose.

The Cowboy quietly left the premises before the CID officers had time to turn upon him and express in no uncertain terms their profound opinion of Special Branch and any intelligence emanating therefrom.

Some weeks later the proprietor presented the police with a bill for repairs to the doors of his guest house and for months this bill circulated between Special Branch and the CID as each claimed the other should pay the damages. Eventually, the poor proprietor decided that it was a hopeless prospect and gave up.

Chapter Sixteen

THE WASTED AFTERNOON

The Cowboy sat alone in the corner of the Italian restaurant toying with a half-full glass of Irish coffee whilst waiters bustled around the empty tables laying up in preparation for the evening and cast occasional glances at the Gwai Lo (devil man or foreigner) to encourage him to drink up and leave.

Glancing through the shaded windows he could see a row of Wanchai bars across the road which somehow looked forlorn and dingy in the harsh light of day. Partially raised metal grilles fronted many of the bars and he half imagined a pall of stale cigarette smoke and rancid beer fumes drifting out into the street as the staff cleaned out in preparation for another day. In years now gone there had been strict licensing laws and all the bars opened promptly at 10 am and closed at 2 am with the result that illegal instant membership clubs had flourished to cater for the crowds who wished to continue drinking until dawn. Now the bars could open at any hour of the day or night with the result that most did not open until 8 pm and closed around 3 am and there were no illegal clubs. He smiled to himself at the quirks of human nature and wondered what had happened to the dedicated drinkers of old.

He swallowed some more Irish coffee but it did not kill the after taste of the rough Chianti he had drunk with his meal. Groaning quietly at the gurgling protests from his full stomach, he signalled for his bill and groaned more audibly at the price, particularly that of the six Irish coffees he had put away.

He stepped down into the street and walked slowly to the

corner of Lockhart Road. The clouds hung low over Victoria Peak and the air in the concrete jungle below was still and humid. He could already feel the pinpricks of sweat forming on his body and for a fleeting moment considered returning to his air-conditioned office but it would be a sin almost bordering upon sacrilege to give up one of his all too infrequent rest days. He could spend the afternoon in one of the hotel bars but that would be expensive and in any event then he would be in no fit state for a late night on the town with his colleagues.

A massage seemed a good idea so he hailed a taxi but with little success as most of those loitering in Fenwick Street were waiting for a return trip to Kowloon. After a little gentle persuasion one taxi driver agreed to take him to King's Road in North Point where there was a reasonable massage parlour.

The hostess in the ground floor lobby greeted him with familiarity and ushered him into the lift which exclusively served the massage parlour on the third floor. It was a simple arrangement which allowed the hostess to vet all incoming clients and give early warning of any visit from the local Vice Squad. On the third floor two more hostesses dressed in figure hugging old-fashioned cheung shaams with hip-length slits greeted him as an old friend since few foreigners frequented the establishment and even fewer spoke fluent street Cantonese. They were well aware that he was probably a Chai Lo (police officer) but no one ever mentioned the fact.

He locked his belongings away in a locker and, slipping the elastic key ring over his wrist, wandered into the steam room. He worked up a profuse sweat over the next fifteen minutes then emerged and took a cool shower before repeating the exercise. He contemplated the two jacuzzi pools but once again could not pluck up the courage to plunge into the ice-cold water, it would be just too big a shock to his system. Anyway, he was now feeling a little better so he dried off and allowed the male attendant to help him into a pair of baggy shorts and a loose gown before wandering into the lounge.

Settling down in a large soft armchair he ordered a large cold orange juice on the grounds that Vitamin C was healthy. Lola, the manageress, was tall for a Cantonese and her height was accentuated by 4-inch heels and hair piled up on top of her head. She produced the check list showing the numbers of the masseuses available at that time and the Cowboy inquired if she herself was available, commenting that she was by far the most attractive female on the premises. It was an old joke between them but Lola never failed to blush slightly and suggest that perhaps next time he came.

Lola suggested a couple of numbers then pointed to another number and said that this one was a recent arrival from Shanghai who had a very good figure and gave good service but would not be available for about thirty minutes. The Cowboy was in no hurry so he agreed with her suggestion then settled back in his chair and had a cigarette whilst he watched an old Cantonese film starring Lin Dai and Peter Cheung.

Some thirty minutes later an attendant came and escorted him through a labyrinth of cubicles to the one allocated to him. The cubicles, constructed of hardboard partitions, were highly functional in their simple design being about ten feet square with two massage couches and a folding partition between them to provide some degree of privacy when in double occupation. Two stools and an internal telephone on a small table which was littered with half empty bottles of body oil and talcum powder completed the furnishings. He sat on the couch finishing off a last cigarette and a minute or so later the girl from Shanghai entered.

She was tall and slender with her long hair drawn back in a ponytail which showed her facial features to advantage. She was wearing shorts and a loose fitting T-shirt which only served to emphasize her well developed breasts. She seemed a little taken aback on seeing a Gwai Lo in the room and her concern was apparent when she called in on the house phone to report her arrival. Turning back to the Cowboy she introduced herself in a fractured mixture of Shanghaiese, English and Cantonese and within moments communication was established between them. She carefully folded towels around the head space at the top of the couch and without prompting the Cowboy climbed on the couch and positioned himself with his face resting in the nest of towels.

The girl straddled him, poured some body oil on his back then started to massage him with her surprisingly strong fingers. The Cowboy could not help but be aware of her naked inner thighs rubbing against his waist and it took little imagination to realize which part of her body was running up and down the small of his spine. After massaging the back of his legs she tugged the shorts he was wearing and, after he had eased himself up slightly, she slipped them down over his legs. She poured more oil over the small of his back and buttocks and started massaging again, but this time using the tips of her fingers so that it felt like the fluttering of feathers on his skin. The oil ran down between the cheeks of his buttocks and her exploring fingers followed the oil as far as his scrotum. His muscles twitched in sexual anticipation as her fingers became more and more familiar with his private parts. She tapped him on the shoulder and gestured that he should turn over. As he did he noticed her putting her hand up the front of her T-shirt and releasing her bra clip.

The girl leaned over him. Her fingers dancing lightly down over his stomach found his manhood which responded quickly to the teasing fingers. She murmured quietly, but when he did not respond she took his hand and guided it under her T-shirt to her naked breast. After a moment he could feel her nipple responding to his touch and this time he needed no assistance in interpreting her gasped murmurs. She raised her T-shirt exposing her full well-formed breasts and leaning forward offered one to his mouth which he accepted readily.

185

Within moments he shuddered with sexual satisfaction and sagged back on the coach in complete relaxation. The girl smiled and, after adjusting her clothes, left the cubicle. A minute or so later she returned armed with steaming hot towels and started to gently wipe his whole body to take off the oil. She draped a towel over his midriff then moved to the top of the couch and gently massaged his head and face until the internal telephone signalled that the massage period was over.

After the masseuse left the cubicle the Cowboy remained lying on the couch in a form of suspended animation until the shrill of the house telephone brought him back to reality. He slipped the gown back on and returned to the steam room, to sweat off the last vestiges of the body oil, followed by a cool shower. He dressed slowly and after settling the account with a suitable tip for the masseuse he left the establishment.

It was approaching 5 pm when he reached the street again and he felt refreshed and ready for a night on the town. There was the added advantage that the afternoon session had taken the edge of his appetite so that he was less likely to succumb to the charms of any of the ladies of the night that he might encounter in the Wanchai bars. That was no small consideration now that the ladies drinks, usually a small lime and soda, cost $220 each.

Chapter Seventeen

CHINA WATCHING

The Cowboy had already served on the Sino-Hong Kong Border twice in his Uniform Branch service and had lived in the New Territories so, in many ways, it was a strangely logical decision for him to be posted to the Special Branch group responsible for the New Territories and in particular the Sino-Hong Kong Border.

In 1981 the Group Headquarters was located in the then Gurkha Field Force Headquarters at Sek Kong which was convenient for liaison with Army Intelligence and also provided good security. The personnel in the Intelligence Corps were proud of their green berets and it amused the Cowboy that the Cantonese term for a green hat – Luk Mo – was a local colloquialism for a man whose spouse was cheating on him.

After twenty years in Hong Kong and marriage to a Chinese the Cowboy thought that he had acquired a fairly deep knowledge of China and Chinese customs but he was soon brought down to earth by his subordinates and realized that his knowledge was but a drop in a vast ocean. Luckily, he had two good tutors in Michael LEUNG who held an Honours Degree in Chinese history and Sandy LEE who studied Chinese history as a hobby. They were not slow to point out that China has a recorded civilized history reaching back several thousand years, much further than that of any modern Western country. The Chinese were wearing silks when the Cowboy's ancestors lived in caves and dressed in animal skins. They had metal armour and weapons long before the so-called

Bronze Age, had a basic form of printing long before Marco Polo brought the concept back to Europe and used gunpowder long before Guy Fawkes ever dreamed of blowing up the Houses of Parliament. Napoleon showed great foresight when he warned of the dangers of waking the sleeping giant that was China.

China covers a territory of just over three and a half million square miles. It is only slightly larger than the United States of America yet it has a population of well over one billion, which is almost five times that of the United States. The official policy of one child per family was introduced in an attempt to curb the staggering annual increases in population, forecast to exceed two billion within two decades, which would result in famine and deprivation on an extensive scale as the basically agrarian society in China could not hope to support such a population.

In the rural areas cognizance is taken of the need for male children and if the first-born is a girl the policy is not strictly enforced in respect of a second child. In the next two decades there is going to be a predominantly male generation and thereafter natural circumstances will control the rise in population. Naturally, such a policy is anathema in term of human rights and civil liberties and could not be imposed in any civilized Western democracy, but in terms of benefit for China as a nation it is certainly better than the alternative.

There is an old Chinese proverb which translates as 'The prime necessity of a Nation is its population but the prime necessity of the population is food'. A former Professor of Economics at Cambridge University, Dr Malthus, is reported to have once said, 'At any given time in the development of a progressive Country the growth in population increases at a greater rate than the increase of means of subsistence until it is checked by wars, famines or birth control.' History, even that of this century, appears to validate this observation. It is not improbable that China has chosen a more humane solution to its potential problems that some people would allow.

It is only in the last decade that there has been a concerted effort to develop one common language throughout China and now some sixty per cent of the population speak a simplified form of the ancient Mandarin termed 'Putunghua' (Common Speech). In the seventies it was claimed in a study by Hong Kong University that there were eighty-seven distinct languages spoken in China, aside from several hundred local dialects. This is not, perhaps, a surprise as China is a country where time has stood still for several centuries and, even in the first half of this century, China remained a feudalistic state ruled largely by local 'Robber Barons' who paid occasional homage to the Nationalist government.

Only in the last forty years under the somewhat despotic rule of the Chinese Communist Party has there been a positive attempt to drag China into the modern industrial world. The grandiose Five Year Plans and the 'Great Leap Forward' introduced by Chairman Mao were simplistic and idealist efforts doomed to failure by the very environment into which they were introduced. The more pragmatic approach proposed by DEN Xiaoping in 1978 concentrating on the modernization of agriculture, industry, science/technology and national defence – more commonly referred to as the 'The Four Modernizations' – appears to be achieving a significant degree of success, though not without some aberrations.

Some ninety per cent of the people in China are of the Han Race, but for most of the last 2,000 years central government has been in the hands of minority or foreign races. The first period of Han Rule over an united China was from 206 BC to AD 220 but then Chins divided it into the Three Kingdoms. Internal strife between the Three Kingdoms allowed the Turkic speaking Tobas from Toba on the northern border of China to establish their ascendancy and they and their descendants, the Sui and the Tang Dynasties, ruled an united China for the following three centuries. During this period the Tobas were assimilated into the Han Race and the nomadic Toba Tribe ceased to have a separate identity, though in some remote parts of northern China the language still exists. With the fall of the Tang Dynasty the country was once again split into a number of semi-independent feudal states under the nominal rules of the Northern and later the Southern Song Dynasties.

In 1211 Genghis Khan and his Mongol hordes invaded China but it took his grandson Kublai Khan to complete the conquest in 1279. Mongol rule over an united China lasted less than 100 years before civil wars broke out which eventually led to the establishment of the Ming Dynasty, which at least brought stability for the next three centuries. The Ming Emperors generally pursued a policy of 'splendid isolation' and supported the concept that China was culturally and economically superior to the rest of the world which was populated by barbarians, a concept that is ingrained in the Chinese psyche to this day.

In the mid seventeenth century came the Manchu invasion of China and the establishment of the Quin Dynasty which lasted until the death of the Dowager Empress Ci Xi in 1908 and the establishment of the largely token government of the Nationalist Republic of China in 1911. War-lords governed large tracts of China independent of central government control and the Nationalist government had no independent army under its direct control to enforce its authority. Civil unrest and minor civil wars continued for the next twenty years until the emergence of the Chinese Communist Party as a major political and military force compelled the War-lords to choose sides and even they changed sides frequently during the following thirty years of civil war and war with Japan. Eventually the Chinese Communist Party, with the support of uneducated masses from the countryside, prevailed and the People's Republic of China was established in 1949.

In the sixteenth century the Europeans started to arrive in China by sea and in 1557 the Portuguese established their

Colony of Macau at the mouth of the Pearl River on the south coast of China. Shortly afterwards the British, Dutch and Spanish seafarers arrived in the China Seas and many were based in Macau for their trading. The Qing government attempted to keep Westerners out of China in pursuance of their isolationist policy, but Westerners were not to be denied, particularly the British, who became deeply involved in the opium trade (foreign mud) and were prepared to mount military expeditions in support of their right to trade in opium.

In 1839 the Qing government banned the import of opium to China and a large quantity of opium was seized on the docks of Guangzhou and burned in public. The following year the British retaliated by sending a naval expeditionary force up the Pearl River which laid waste to the small ports of Xiamen, Dinghai and Tianjin forcing the Qing government to sue for peace. Qi Shan, Viceroy of Hebei, agreed to demolish the defence walls around Guangzhou, indemnify the British for the loss of the burned opium and to allow them to occupy Hong Kong as a trade base. On 2nd February 1841 Captain Charles Elliot proclaimed the victory and the establishment of the Colony of Hong Kong.

However, Emperor DAO Guang refused to ratify the terms of the peace agreement whilst Lord Palmerston as Prime Minister in England was equally cool in his reception of the news that a barren rock on the coast of China had been proclaimed a Colony. A further naval expedition forced entry into the port of Humen and Admiral Guan Tianpei was killed in the skirmish with some 400 men. Three months later an armistice was signed after the Qing government paid an indemnity to the British not to lay waste the port of Guanzhou.

On 29th August 1842 the original peace agreement was ratified under the terms of the Treaty of Nanjing which ceded the Colony of Hong Kong to the British in perpetuity whilst the ports of Guangzhou, Xiamen Fuzhou, Ningbo and Shanghai were declared open to foreign trade and a further indemnity of twenty-one million silver dollars was paid to the British. The United States, which had also landed an expeditionary force in China, obtained the right to engage in coastal trade and establish consular presence in the open ports under the terms of the Treaty of Wanghia signed in 1844. In the meantime the French, under the terms of the Treaty of Whampoa, also obtained trade rights and the right to propagate Roman Catholicism in China.

In October 1856 a British registered lighter was seized in Guangzhou and the following year a French Catholic Father, Pére Chapdelaine, was murdered in Guangxi which resulted in a combined British and French expeditionary force being launched against Guangzhou in December 1857. The city was occupied in early 1858 as was Dagu in April 1858 and Tianjin in May 1858. At this time both the Russians and the Americans were lending support to the British and French forces and the Qing government was forced to accede to the terms of the Sino-British, Sino-French, Sino-American and Sino-Russian Treaties of Tiensin. Under the terms of these treaties the British and French were again paid indemnities, the six coastal ports of Nuzhuang, Dengzhou, Tainan, Danshui, Chaozhou and Qiongzhou and the river ports of Hankou, Jiujiang, Nanjing and Zhenjiang declared open to foreign trade. Freedom was granted to propagate other Western religions and Western warships were given right of entry to various ports.

In January 1851, HONG Xiuquan, a Chinese Christian from Guangdong Province, launched what came to be called the 'Taiping Revolution' which slowly gathered momentum and by 1860 the Taiping Christian Army held sway over much of southern China. The Christian Taiping banned gambling, prostitution and opium which did not please the Western powers. In 1860 the Qing government sought the assistance of the Western powers to put down the Taiping Revolution and French, American and British forces came to their aid. British troops under the command of General 'Chinese'

Gordon and American troops under Colonel Ward combined to form the 'Ever Victorious Army' which engaged the Taiping army whilst French troops took the field against the Taiping forces in Zhejiang Province. In July 1864 the last of the Taiping forces were defeated at Nanjing and Qing rule over China was again stabilized. In return the Qing government conceded further trade concessions and legalized the trade in opium. The British gained the Kowloon Peninsula as an extension of the Colony of Hong Kong.

During the next forty years expeditionary forces were launched into China at various times by the British, Japanese, French, German, American and Russian governments to protect their trade interests and extend their 'Spheres of Influence'. In April 1874 a joint American and Japanese force landed on Taiwan whilst in 1876 under the Chefoo Convention the British gained the right to extend trade into Yunan, Sichuan, Tibet, Qinghai and Gansu. The Germans established control over most of Shandong Province and the Russians annexed the area north of the Heilongjiang River and part of Xinjiang Province.

In 1895 under the Treaty of Shimonoseki the Liaodong Peninsula, Taiwan and the Penghu Islands were ceded to Japan and Chinese ports were opened to Japan. In the same year the French incorporated part of Yunan Province into Indo-Chine (now Vietnam) whilst the British also sought to obtain Yerenshan in Yunan Province to counter the French and Weihaiwei in Shandong Province to counter the Russians.

In 1898 the British leased an extension of the Colony of Hong Kong now referred to as the New Territories whilst the Russians obtained the lease of Lushan and Dalian in the same year. In fact the only Western power not to gain control of territory was America which sought a general 'Open Door Policy' in which all powers had access to all ceded or leased lands. At the close of the nineteenth century the Western powers were scrambling to extend their 'Spheres of Influence' and divide China on similar lines to the colonization of Africa a century earlier.

The Yi He Tuan (Boxers of Righteous Harmony) was originally a secret or triad society based in Shandong Province and its members honoured Chinese tradition, particularly Chinese martial arts, hence they became known to the West as the 'Boxers'. In the late nineteenth century the Yi He Tuan had expanded into many parts of China and gained influence for its support of Chinese tradition and opposition to Western influence. Attacks on Westerners increased, possibly with the tacit approval of the Qing government, leading to what is now referred to as the Boxer Revolution of 1900. This was put down by combined British, American, Russian, French, German, Japanese, Italian and Austrian forces which claimed to be acting in support of the legitimate government of China.

In 1908 the Empress Dowager died, the 2-year-old Emperor Puyi ascended to the throne and the remnants of power held by the central government rapidly fell apart. The Alliance for Chinese Revolution led by Dr SUN Yatsen gathered greater support from the wealthy middle classes and in 1911 there was a military revolt in Wuhan which sparked a country-wide declaration of dissatisfaction with the Qing rule.

On 1st January 1912 Dr SUN Yatsen was proclaimed President of the Republic of China but it was a rather symbolic position; power in China was now fragmented as various War-lords jostled for power. A major player, YUAN Shikai, former Chief of the Imperial Army, dominated a large area of the north. During World War I the Japanese entertained ideas of taking over China as a colony while the other major colonial powers were otherwise occupied.

The Treaty of Versailles awarded the former German colonies in China to Japan and this proved to be the catalyst to the Chinese as a wave of nationalist pride mounted on an anti-foreign intervention swept through China. SUN Yatsen and his Kuomintang were a major political force and were supported by the fledgling Marxist groups in Tianjin (Zhou Enlai) Heibei (LIN Biao) and Beijing (MAO Zedong). The Chinese Communist Party was formed in 1921 and the collaboration continued until the death of Dr SUN Yatsen in 1925 and in the subsequent jockeying for power the alliance ceased.

CHIANG Kaishek emerged as the Kuomintang leader and by 1928 had established a seat of government in Beijing with both military and political power in his grasp. However, the 1927 massacre of Communist supporters in Shanghai had served to unite the various factions of the Chinese Communist Party with MAO Zedong emerging as the dominant leader. In the ensuing civil war the mainly peasant Communist armies were hard pressed by the relatively well armed Nationalist armies and by 1933 were on the brink of final defeat, but the Nationalists were diverted from their objective by the expansionist plans of Japan who occupied Manchuria in 1931.

During 1934 the remnants of the various Communist armies regrouped and made their way in a series of 'Long Marches' in Shaanxi. The most famous of these 'Long Marches' was the march from Jiangxi Province to Shaanxi a distance of over 5,000 miles which took a year to complete; of the nearly 100,000 who started less than 20,000 reached their destination. However, it served to bring together and forge a close bond between the nucleus of the leaders of the Chinese Communist Party.

In 1937 the Japanese launched an all-out invasion of China and overran large tracts of the country which brought an uneasy truce in the civil war. At the end of World War II the civil war broke out again and by 1949 CHIANG Kaishek had taken refuge with the remnants of his army on Formosa whilst the new People's Republic of China was proclaimed in Beijing on 1st October 1949.

A recurring theme throughout history is of a country experiencing conditions of extreme hardship, poverty or generally incompetent government that seems to produce a strong, autocratic leader who takes the country forward into a period of great success then falls from power in disgrace. Bismarck united the Germanic peoples and brought Germany to the forefront of Europe then fell from power. Hitler repeated the exercise then fell as did Mussolini with Italy. In the fifties De Gaulle provided the necessary leadership to bring France out of the political and economic doldrums and in the seventies Marcos did the same with the Philippines.

In the case of China it was MAO Zedong who provided the autocratic leadership that brought war-torn and fragmented China belatedly into the twentieth century. It was a momentous task and, to a large extent, it must be admitted that he succeeded although not at the pace nor to the extent he had envisaged. The Cultural Revolution between 1966 and 1976 was an attempt to go against human nature and produce a genuinely classless society but in fact was a disaster of huge proportions. All persons with any form of academic background were purged and schools were closed as pupils were 'sent down to the countryside' to learn the basics of husbandry. All forms of property ownership were made illegal and everyone from the lowly uneducated peasant hill farmer to the university professor was declared to be equal in status and salary. Even now, some thirty years later, the effects of a country being in chaos for a decade are still apparent.

It is a remarkable achievement that China seems to have recovered so well and, in terms of economic growth and industrial development, has reached its present position as a major world power.

Chapter Eighteen

A PERSPECTIVE OF TIANANMEN
SQUARE

One of the more famous adages attributed to MAO Zedong was that political power came from the barrel of a gun and whilst this is valid in many instances MAO overlooked an equally potent source of power – students.

The university student, existing in an unrealistic and academic environment, absorbs a wealth of abstract theories and ideals, then with naive enthusiasm ventures into the real world with the conviction that he has discovered the solutions to all the major problems that beset the world. It is only later as he matures he realizes that all he is attempting to do is re-invent the wheel. However, for a period the student is a potent political weapon and when student enthusiasm is collectively marshalled it has on occasion brought the downfall of authority. MAO Zedong, himself, used the power of students with his Red Guards to bring about the Cultural Revolution in China in 1966.

After ten years of Cultural Revolution it was apparent to most people in China that the movement was a failure but the public admission of failure would be a loss of national face, an attack on JIANG Qing and an admission of error on the part of the Great Helmsman. In January 1976 ZHOU Enlai died and his death became the catalyst for change. Mourning the death of ZHOU became a symbol of support for change and during the Qing Ming Festival in March many people came to Tiananmen Square to honour ZHOU according to Chinese tradition.

The concept caught the imagination of the students and

each day more and more people gathered in Tiananmen Square to pay homage to ZHOU. By 5th April the daily gathering had reached tens of thousands and was now being viewed by the central government with some consternation. The possibility that the situation was or could be utilized by DENG Ziaoping in his struggle to regain power could not be ignored and the PLA were called out to disperse the mourners. Accounts of events of 5th April in Tiananmen Square are vague but it seems likely that many of the mourners were killed or imprisoned. An object lesson to those in power and to those who protested, however obliquely.

As the reverberations of the Cultural Revolution receded, the Chinese leadership particularly DENG Xiapeng, HU Yaobang and ZHAO Ziyang, accepted that the previous, isolationist, agrarian policies were not compatible with the demands of a booming population in the modern world. In December 1978, at the Third Plenum of the Eleventh Party Committee of the Chinese Communist Party held in Beijing, a commitment was made to achieve the modernization of agriculture, industry, science/technology and defence – often termed the 'Four Modernizations'. This entailed the abandonment of the country-wide commune system, the encouragement of links with the West in order to obtain financial investments and the benefits of the latest Western technology and encouraging overseas Chinese to return to the Motherland. There was significant opposition from those who still adhered to the maxims of MAO Zedong and power struggles continued to dominate the machinations of the Central Party Committee for many years.

The dangers of Western influence or 'spiritual pollution' were recognized and attempts were made to curtail its effect but the exposure to Western ideals and concepts spread, particularly as more and more overseas Chinese returned to China and more students educated in the West, particularly in the United States, came home again. The changes brought greater freedom and autonomy for the masses and even a form of capitalism, with the emergence of 'Independent Business Operators', was encouraged.

It was a natural progression for freedom and affluence to stimulate desires for even greater freedom and greater affluence. In the universities around China these desires fermented and there was a growing impatience and discontent on many campuses. The first public manifestations of this unrest came in December 1986 at the China Science and Technology University in Hefei the provincial capital of Anhui Province; students took to the streets to protest about the election practices for the Provincial People's Congress. The unrest spread to Shanghai where an estimated 10,000 students crowded the streets on 19th December to demand greater freedom and democracy and the following day their numbers swelled to over 50,000. The news of the unrest quickly spread and within days students took to the streets in Kunming, Nanjing, Tianjin and even in the small Special Economic Zone of Shenzhen adjacent to Hong Kong. By the end of the month the students in Beijing were on the march and several thousand staged a token 'sit-in' in Tiananmen Square.

Generally, the protests fizzled out without any violent confrontation with the authorities but the protests brought about the downfall of HU Yaobang, the Communist Party General Secretary, on the grounds that he had failed to take steps to prevent the spread of 'bourgeois liberalization' on the campuses. The China Science and Technology University had benefitted significantly from the relaxed control on links with the West, particularly the United States. Perhaps reports of its students quoting excerpts from Lincoln's Gettysburg Address can be given credence. Certainly FANG Lizhi, astrophycist and Vice-President of the University, did not discourage the students in his addresses to them in November 1986, in which he disparaged China's Communist socialist system and urged students to be a progressive force for democracy.

What no one foresaw was that the student protests of 1976 and then of 1986 would set in motion the train of events leading to the unfortunate confrontation in Tiananmen Square in June 1989.

Article 33 to Article 56 of the Constitution of the People's Republic of China set out the Fundamental Rights and Duties of Citizens. The students in their protest actions relied for their protection upon the provisions of Article 35 which reads:

Article 35. Citizens of the People's Republic of China enjoy freedom of speech, of the press, of assembly, of association, of procession and of demonstration.

However, in so doing they tended to overlook the provisions of other Articles such as:

Article 51. Citizens of the People's Republic of China, in exercising their freedoms and rights, may not infringe upon the interests of the State, of society or of the collective, or upon the lawful freedoms and rights of other citizens.

Article 53. Citizens of the People's Republic of China must abide by the Constitution and the Law, keep State secrets, protect public property, observe labour discipline and public order and respect social ethics.

Article 54. It is the duty of citizens of the People's Republic of China to safeguard the security, honour and interests of the Motherland; they must not commit acts detrimental to the security, honour and interests of the Motherland.

In February 1989 President Bush took advantage of the requirement to be in Tokyo for the funeral of Emperor Hirohito to make a hastily arranged visit to China. This was a political expedient that followed swiftly upon the heels of a visit to China by Soviet Foreign Minister Eduard Shevardnadze and the announcement of the State visit by the Soviet General Secretary Mikhail Gorbachev in May 1986. The Chinese authorities were not happy about United States support for dissidents in China and ZHAO Zhiyang raised this issue in his meeting with Bush. However, the United States decided to ignore Chinese sensitivity on the subject and gave public support to the dissidents by inviting FANG Lizhi and his wife LI Shuxian to a barbecue hosted at the Sheraton Great Wall Hotel by President Bush. The Chinese viewed this with obvious displeasure in a reaction not dissimilar to that of John Major when President Clinton invited Gerry Adams to the White House.

On 15th April 1989 HU Yaobang died and a funeral service for him was to be held in the Great Hall of the People on 22nd April. HU had been removed from office following the student unrest in 1986 and students identified him with their aspirations so, as previously with the death of ZHOU Enlai, the death of HU was the catalyst for an outbreak of student unrest on campuses throughout the country. Students took to the streets in their thousands in Shanghai, Nanjing, Tsinjin, Wuhan, Hefei and, of course, in Beijing.

On 18th April some 10,000 students gathered in Tiananmen Square and staged a day-long sit-in in front of the Great Hall of the People. The first signs of political overtones surfaced when some 3,000 students besieged the Communist Party Headquarters at Zhongnanhai to demand the rehabilitation of HU and the resignation of the Party Central Committee. After minor scuffles the students were dispersed without major incident.

Over 30,000 students returned to Tiananmen Square on the 19th April and this time the scuffles were more violent with injuries sustained by both students and police. In typical Chinese fashion students took to breaking small bottles as a symbol of their anger towards DENG Ziaoping – the significance being that the Chinese words for 'breaking small bottles' sound similar to that name. Over 100,000 students gathered in Tiananmen Square on 21st April to pay homage to HU but it soon degenerated into an anti-government demonstration with demands for greater freedom and reform of government.

Initially, the authorities intended to restrict access to Tiananmen Square on 22nd April to maintain the solemnity of the official mourning ceremony as they were aware of the adverse image the student demonstrations would create. Around 50,000 students remained in the square overnight, which pre-empted any design to restrict access and eventually over 200,000 students gathered in the square to pay their noisy homage during the official ceremony. Once again, as the day ended, the police eventually dispersed the students without any violent confrontation, though there were reports of violence in other parts of China.

Instead of settling down after the official ceremonies, the student protests gathered momentum throughout the country. In Beijing the students expressed their dissatisfaction with the existing student bodies and the Independent Students' Union of Beijing University was established with ZHOU Yongjun as president. At the same time student protests escalated in Shanghai, Nanjing and Chengdu. In Beijing the students were somewhat indecisive about their future actions and, following a meeting with HE Dongchang, Vice-Minister of the State Education Committee, and YUAN Mu, a Vice-Minister, ZHOU Yongjun cancelled the demonstration planned for 27th April.

On 26th April DENG Xiaoping condemned the student protests whilst the *People's Daily* printed an article highly critical of the students' activities. This had the effect of galvanizing the students' resolve and ZHOU was replaced as student president by Wuer Kaixi of the United Association of Beijing University Students who, in turn, was replaced within three days by FENG Conde, the husband of CHAI Ling. The planned demonstration for 27th April went ahead and some 200,000 students and supporters forced their way onto Tiananmen Square and remained there throughout the day.

On lst May the students called a press conference where FENG Conde made his appearance as the new President of the Independent Students' Union and WANG Dan, a student of FENG Lizhi, emerged as a student leader. On 2nd May representatives of the students delivered an ultimatum to the National People's Congress which demanded official recognition of the new student bodies, freedom of assembly and an amnesty in respect of student activities to that time. Failing that, there would be a major protest in Tiananmen Square on the 4th May which would coincide with the meeting in the Great Hall of the People of the Asian Development Bank.

On 4th May the students broke through the police barrier and again occupied Tiananmen Square but eventually they dispersed peacefully and ZHAO Ziyang in his address to the World Development Bank that evening implied that the differences with the students had been resolved. In the following days it did appear that conciliation was possible since most of the Beijing students returned to their studies and ZHAO appointed LI Tieying of the State Education Commission to negotiate with student leaders. That still left the students from other universities who had flooded into Beijing over the previous weeks. An added ingredient was the host of Western media representatives who had descended upon Beijing to cover the Sino-Soviet Summit. They thought that, in the student demonstrations, with recent events in Moscow in their minds, they were now witnessing the downfall of the Communist regime. It is not clear what, if any, influence the Western media had on events but their frequent visits to Tiananmen Square certainly served to revive the students' morale when it flagged.

The negotiations between the student leaders and the

government representatives reached a stalemate and on 13th May the students returned to Tiananmen Square in their thousands. At first the proposal to resume the demonstration had not met with much support, but CHAI Ling made an impassioned speech which became the manifesto for the student movement and tape recordings of the speech were sent to universities throughout the country. ZHAO Ziyang appealed to the students not to jeopardize political and social stability in China and to protect the international prestige of China but was ignored, as was CHEN Xitong, Mayor of Beijing, when he visited Tiananmen Square on the morning of 14th May.

Late in the afternoon of 14th May FENG Conde raised a banner with Chinese characters reading 'Hunger Strike' and so the hunger strike commenced and with it a commitment to remain in Tiananmen Square until the protest was resolved. Although the Chinese authorities announced that the square was to be cleared in advance of the arrival of Mikhail Gorbachev, no attempt was made to disperse the students, but under the guidance of Wuer Kaixi the hunger strikers moved to the eastern side of the square, away from the Great Hall of the People where the welcoming ceremony was due to take place. The ceremony in fact was transferred to Beijing Airport to avoid any confrontation with the students.

Early on the morning of 15th May the numbers in the square had dwindled to a few thousand but by early afternoon the students and their supporters returned in large numbers. YAN Mingfu of the Party Central Committee tried to negotiate with the student leaders but this exercise was fraught with difficulty as positive cohesive leadership had yet to crystallize and there were many factions among the students. Late that night a breakaway faction of some 60,000 protesters tried to force their way into the Great Hall of the People but were dissuaded at the last moment by CHAI Ling and LI Lu. By 16th May the crowds in the square had grown to over 1,000,000 and the number of students fasting to over 3,000. Emotions ran high among the students and after less than three days of fasting over 300 students had collapsed and been taken to hospital by ambulance.

During that afternoon DENG Xiaoping held a meeting with Mikhail Gorbachev in the Great Hall of the People and both leaders had to arrive and leave through the back entrance to avoid any confrontation with the students. In the evening YUAN Mingfu came to talk with the student leaders and appealed for an end of the hunger strike, even offering to become a hostage for the safety of the students. Some of the student leaders such as Wuer Kaixi agreed that the hunger strike should end, but after several hours of discussion no decision could be reached.

At midnight ZHAO Ziyang put his own political future on the line by issuing a statement affirming the patriotic spirit of the students, promising reforms in government and that the Chinese leaders would engage in constructive talks with the student leaders if the students would return to their campuses. This concession was ignored by the protesters and on 18th May the crowds had grown to almost 2,000,000 in and around Tiananmen Square. That afternoon ZHAO Ziyang and LI Peng visited those students who had been hospitalized and then visited Tiananmen Square before LI Peng held a televised meeting with student leaders in the Great Hall of the People. The acts of conciliation by the Chinese leaders were ignored and on 20th May the crowds were, if anything, even larger around the square.

On 20th May LI Peng lost patience and signed the Order declaring Martial Law in eight central districts of Beijing including Tiananmen Square and military units started moving into the outskirts of Beijing. This was the beginning of the military build-up as the Central Military Commission decided to draw units from various army groups which would provide a cross section of the community rather than have just one racial group involved. This also ensured that adequate strength remained in their bases to deal with localized problems as by this time disturbances had broken out in over twenty cities. The speed and efficiency with which this logistic task was carried out surprised many Western military observers. In response, the protesters set up road-blocks on all the roads leading into Tiananmen Square.

Over a million people demonstrated in and around Tiananmen Square on 23rd May demanding the resignations of LI Peng and DENG Xiaoping but there was still no positive reaction from the Chinese authorities, who appeared to have problems of dissension within their own ranks, and by 26th May it was clear that ZHAO Ziyang had been removed from his post of Party General Secretary. In Tiananmen Square there was also disorder within the ranks and opinions were divided as to whether or not to continue the protests. On 22nd May the leadership of the student protest was revised after a series of meetings with CHAI Ling, now becoming the commander, and FENG Conde, LI Lu and ZHANG Boli as deputy commanders and other posts given to WANG Dan, BAO Zunxin and ZHANG Ming.

Fatigue, lethargy and discord had reduced the number in the square to less than 1,000 by 27th May. Wuer Kaixi, WANG Dang and CHAI Ling each addressed a news conference and, whilst Wuer Kaixi called for an end to the occupation of Tiananmen Square after one more rally, WANG Dan was more confrontational, issuing a series of demands in the name of the People's Democracy Movement. This seems to have galvanized the student movement, particularly those students who had come from universities in other parts of the country, many of whom wanted to continue the occupation until the next meeting of the National People's Congress on 20th June. At this time there were as many non-students as students in the square, some from the recently established Beijing Autonomous Workers' Union the first independent labour

206

union to be established in China.

On 28th May some 100,000 people gathered in Tiananmen Square to call for the overthrow of LI Peng who had become the focus of their hatred for issuing the Martial Law Order. The student leaders continued to squabble among themselves about the best course of action but none of the factions could agree. On 30th May students from the Central Fine Arts Academy produced the 'Goddess of Democracy', a thirty-foot high styrofoam statue modelled on the American Statue of Liberty and this had the effect of lifting the flagging spirits of the students and bringing a degree of concord to the square.

The appearance of HO Dejian, celebrated pop-singer, on 2nd June attracted close to 500,000 people to the square but now the net was closing and the troops were starting to move in on the square. The barricades erected earlier held out and there were only a few reported violent clashes, though some troops made their way into the Great Hall of the People.

On the afternoon of 3rd June there was the first concerted effort by unarmed troops to clear the square but they were repulsed by the protesters. In the scuffles a number were injured on both sides and for the first time it was apparent that weapons had been stored in the square. A heavy machine-gun was mounted in a sand-bagged position at the base of the Martyr's Monument with light machine-guns in sand-bagged positions above and beside it to provide covering fire.

There was another concerted effort about 11 pm to push the protesters out of the square by unarmed troops and this time the clashes were more violent with one student emptying the magazine of a captured AK 47 into the advancing troops at a range of about twenty-five metres. The troops once again withdrew into the Great Hall of the People and the Summer Palace. During the following hours the sound of tanks and mechanized transport could be heard drawing nearer and it became clear to those in the square that a final confrontation was at hand. Many left quietly whilst others determined to fight on to the last, but once again there was a large degree of indecisiveness among the leaders.

At about 2 am three green Very flares burst over the square and the area was plunged into darkness as all power was cut off. A few minutes later three red Very flares burst over the square and all the light came on to reveal armed troops in position on three sides. The troops started to advance, pushing the protesters before them and behind the troops came the tanks and armoured personnel carriers. The remaining protesters started to panic and streamed to the two lanes which provided the only avenues of escape and it seems quite possible that some fell and were trampled underfoot by their companions.

Certainly there were a numbers of deaths at this time but the dead bodies shown in the subsequent media photographs did not bear injuries consistent with being crunched under the tracks of a tank. One observer later commented that if 90 people could be crushed to death as 2,000 tried to force their way into the Sheffield football ground then one must expect casualties when over 10,000 try to rush into two narrow lanes in semi-darkness and in a state of panic. Undoubtedly some people were crushed under the armoured vehicles but, according to many who were present at the crucial time, the media reports of peacefully sleeping students being crushed in their tents were dramatic overstatements of events.

During the military build-up to the final push there were a number of acts of extreme violence by protesters on the outskirts of Beijing including the blowing up and derailment of a troop train resulting in several hundred casualties, the destruction of several tanks with Molotov cocktails and the public execution of a number of captured soldiers. Following the clearing of Tiananmen Square it seems likely that the troops who had been restrained for so long and who had sustained numerous casualties went on the rampage as they hunted down the fleeing protesters. On 7th June there was a diplomatic protest when troops opened fire on one of the main diplomatic compounds in error, after they had come under fire from a flat in an adjacent block by an armed student who despaired of gaining sanctuary in the diplomatic block.

The student protests in Tiananmen Square initially related to life on the campus and the protests gathered strength at the refusal of the Chinese authorities to recognize the legitimacy of their grievances. Later, the protests developed into a fight for greater democracy, but for the vast majority of the protesters that concept was a vague ideal which they did not fully understand. In the square with the teeming thousands from many parts of China there was little cohesion and great anarchy, even after CHAI Ling established her command headquarters. There was continual bickering among the leaders and even, at one stage, an attempt by one faction to depose FENG Conde by force in the middle of the night.

At no time was there any unified structure and up to the last day people came and left at their own whim with no restriction upon their movement either by the protesters or by the Chinese authorities. For their part there seems to have been a large degree of indecision by the Chinese authorities, attributable partly to a reluctance to commit the PLA in such a public arena and partly to political infighting within the party leadership.

LI Peng raised the issue of Western support for the protesters. Certainly, the presence of such a large number of representatives of the Western media lent support and encouragement to the students, as did the news of the massive marches in Hong Kong and the financial support from Hong Kong. The cost of logistic support for the protest must have been considerable, the feeding of several hundred thousand people each day over a three-week period must have cost a fortune in a country where the average monthly wage is about ten pounds.

209

Whatever else, the events in Tiananmen Square on the morning of 4th June were an avoidable tragedy. The blame does not rest solely on the shoulders of the Chinese leadership but must also be, to some extent, apportioned among those who supported and encouraged the naive young students to carry on when reason dictated that they had gained their initial objective and to continue was courting disaster. Whilst the Chinese leadership was somewhat heavy-handed in their handling of the situation would there be any guarantee that there would not be a similar outcome if there was an armed insurrection in Times Square or Trafalgar Square? Recent incidents in those countries do not support such a guarantee.

In 1932 'Horse and Mechanized Cavalry' under the command of General MacArthur charged and demolished the shanty town built in Anacosta Flats by protesting American Veterans and only three decades ago five protesting students were shot dead by the US National Guard at Kent University. The student protests in Paris in the sixties and the miners' strikes of the eighties in England were also resolved by force though in neither instance were the protesters seeking to overthrow the elected government.

For the last 200 years China has relatively successfully repelled rapacious attempts at colonialization which must be to the credit of the Chinese people and their leaders from the Empress Dowager to DENG Ziaoping. The resultant defensive isolation of China has occasioned lack of social, economic and industrial development which has been accentuated by the sheer size of the country and its population. Any attempt at this stage to forcibly introduce a form of Western-style democracy would result in complete anarchy and a breakdown of the limited law and order that currently exists, as has happened in many former colonies and more recently in the former Yugoslavia.

Democracy can not be implemented in a few weeks or

months but needs to be nurtured and developed over several decades. It is not the production of instant coffee from a jar but the planting of the coffee seeds, nurturing of the seedlings, cultivation of the plants, gathering the crop and the final production of coffee before the coffee is ready for public consumption. China is already more democratic than it was a mere twenty years ago and has an acceptable Constitution but it must be allowed to develop slowly, without untoward interference from the West in its internal affairs, into an acceptable form of Asian democracy. Any attempt to impose a Western-style democracy by force or intimidation is doomed to failure.

Chapter Nineteen

AFTERMATH OF TIANANMEN SQUARE

When the Sino-Hong Kong Border was established in 1898 it followed the natural features of the Shenzhen River in the west and the Sha Hei River in the east, which created a number of local problems not least in the small fishing village of Shataukok on the mouth of the Sha Hei River. This river has to all intents dried up and all that remains is a storm nullah running under the main street which, appropriately, is now called Chung Ying Street, loosely translated as Chinese-English Street.

To resolve these anomalies the treaty included a provision that inhabitants of the area could freely cross the Border to tend to their fields and market their products and these were termed the Tolerated Border Crossers.

A further anomaly was that originally China retained sovereignty over the Kowloon Walled City, located near what is now Hong Kong International Airport, and a Right of Passage by land and sea to the Walled City. In time this latter right evolved into the Right of Entry into Hong Kong for up to seventy-five persons per day who were referred to as Exit Permit Holders and given exit permits by the Chinese authorities. In the sixties and seventies these Exit Permit Holders were generally non-productive members of society whom the Chinese authorities were happy to pass on to the more welfare conscious Hong Kong.

In the eighties there was a change in attitude and the Exit Permit Holders generally became younger and more able. A change which the more cynical of the 'Border Watchers' attributed to an early anticipation of the change in sovereignty scheduled for 1997. In addition, there was a steady flow of illegal border crossers termed Illegal Immigrants who, in the main, were seeking the economic advantages offered by Hong Kong and when caught were summarily repatriated to China.

Officers under the command of the Cowboy cultivated the Tolerated Border Crossers and the Exit Permit Holders as sources of low-grade, casual information on conditions in China. On rare occasions information of real interest surfaced, but it did allow the officers to gain a good insight to life in China and how the residents of China perceived their social and economic environment. On occasion an illegal immigrant would claim asylum in Hong Kong and, whilst in normal circumstances this would be a matter for the Immigration Service, the processing of asylum seekers was also a responsibility falling to the Cowboy on the grounds of political sensitivity and practical ability to assess the claims.

The asylum screening exercise was conducted jointly by Army Intelligence and Special Branch officers in a secure facility close to the Border and each passed a report to the Defector Working Group chaired by the Director of Special Branch for a final decision. Asylum seekers had to be processed and the issue resolved within forty-eight hours. A significant difference from the United Kingdom where anyone who requests asylum on landing is released on Social Welfare Benefit for up to twelve months whilst a decision is being reached.

The Cowboy had taken leave in late May 1989 and was lying in the sun on the beach in Phuket blissfully ignorant of the dramatic conclusion to events in Tiananmen Square. On his return to Hong Kong he was agreeably pleased to be met at the plane side by airport colleagues who facilitated his passage through the normal, but irritating, formalities and escorted him to a waiting office car.

On arrival at Headquarters he was briefed on the events in

Tiananmen Square and told that, in anticipation of an influx of democracy activists seeking asylum and the political sensitivity of harbouring such people, a special procedure had been established. A new Select Group had been set up to review asylum claims and would be available at any time of the day or night at one hour's notice to convene a meeting. He, together with selected officers from his unit, would be responsible to the Select Group for the screening and the whole process would have to be completed within twenty-four hours.

Returning to his own office, the Cowboy found that Michael Leung and Sandy LEE had already been briefed and had started to draw up response teams, taking into account dialect abilities and availability of personal transport. Leaving them to get on with the arrangements, the Cowboy started a round of key police districts to brief selected officers on the action to be taken if politically sensitive illegal immigrants were brought into a police station. It was no easy task to arrange since nothing could be committed to writing and the selected officers had to disseminate orders on a need-to-know basis without being specific in detail.

The biggest hurdle proved to be the Army who provided the main security cover over the Border. Army Intelligence officers were somewhat disenchanted at being excluded from the exercise but agreed to act as liaison in respect of any targets arrested by army units on Border Patrol, but the prohibition on any instructions appearing in Daily Orders was an obstacle. In one of the earlier cases the Cowboy was alerted as requested. On his arrival at the army unit he found that just about everyone in the unit was aware of the presence of the target and just about everyone in the Army hierarchy, up to the Commander British Forces, had been informed on an 'informal' basis, which was not the cleverest of beginnings.

In the following weeks an increasing number of escaping dissidents came into the system and team organization to deal with them was soon thrown out of the window as the officers were required to cope with the pressure. These dissidents came from many areas of China, as well as those who had participated in Tiananmen Square, and slowly the officers built up a fairly well detailed picture of the events of April and May in China. With practice they were able to sort out the genuine dissidents from those who were just opportunists.

There had been considerable vocal and financial support for the Pro-Democracy Movement in China from Hong Kong residents. After the 4th June this support became manifest in the formation and funding of an escape orgainization to assist the fleeing dissidents to reach Hong Kong. This was established by John Sham and other leading Democrats in Hong Kong and was given the name Operation Yellow Bird.

Basically, they approached the already well established Triad smuggling operators with a cash offer that could not be refused and the high speed smuggling boats – Taai Fais – with shallow keels and four 250-hp outboard engines which produced speeds in excess of sixty knots were used to bring dissidents across the shallow waters of Mirs Bay in the east or Deep Bay in the west.

Safe houses were set up in various Chinese towns and escorts recruited, often from within the ranks of the Chinese military whose poor salaries made them very susceptible to offers. Operation Yellow Bird became so successful that the Cowboy and his officers were barely able to cope with the flow. There was an even greater problem for the Select Group to arrange the onward passage out of Hong Kong for such numbers so, for one period, the Yellow Bird organizers set up their own safe houses in Hong Kong to hold over dissidents and slow down the flow.

Although the United States government took the high moral ground over Tiananmen Square it was strangely reluctant to provide sanctuary and accept dissidents as refugees other than the high profile leaders, such as CHAI Ling, in whom there was political mileage. The French and Swedish governments, on the other hand, did not join the publicity bandwagon but were far more helpful and assisted the majority of dissidents without asking any questions.

The majority of students, particularly those who had participated in Tiananmen Square, were surprisingly naive in relation to what they had done. Many could spout political slogans and jargon but had little real concept of life outside their own environment. Undoubtedly some were truly motivated by their ideals, to which they adhered with passion, but to others it was just an exciting adventure. It is, therefore, not surprising that within two years many returned to China to continue their studies or to take advantage of their experiences in the West to go into business, in particular as agents for Western business interests.

The tight time constraint did not permit detailed screening of the escapees from China and often the officers relied upon their professional instincts during the screening.

On one occasion the subject answered all the initial, routine questions correctly and had been handed on for a more detailed statement, when one of the officers noticed that the subject's wallet did not feel right. A closer examination showed the stitching to be different on one half and this was unpicked to uncover a Hong Kong Identity Card with the subject's photograph with a different name.

A prolonged and more detailed interview ascertained that the subject was an agent of the Guangdong Provincial Public Security Bureau who had entered Hong Kong some years earlier as an Exit Permit Holder and was now a Hong Kong resident. However, he had been recalled to Guangdong and briefed to infiltrate the Yellow Bird Organization. It might have been possible to charge him with wasting police time but that would have only brought unwarranted publicity and probably a small fine. Repatriation to China would not be legal as he held a Hong Kong Identity Card so there was no alternative but to release him after a nominal forty-eight hours. Urgent efforts were made to alert the Yellow Bird Organization that at least one escape route was blown.

On another occasion the subject answered all the questions correctly but somehow Simon, who was interviewing him, had an uneasy feeling and held him over. The subject, realizing that something was wrong, became uneasy. More pressure was brought to bear including the usual hard-man-soft-man tactic and eventually he confessed that he was in fact a member of the Ministry of State Security tasked with infiltrating the Yellow Bird Organization.

In this instance it was quite easy to arrange his repatriation. This was carried out the following day with the subject travelling in a vehicle separate from those on the routine repatriations and, as the Cowboy discovered later, with a placard around his neck proclaiming his identity. Although only two Chinese government agents were identified during the screening it is not improbable that there were others who were more successful and who may have made their way into the West.

Shortly after the latter incident, a group of seven Public Security Officers from Shekou made their way into Hong Kong in full uniform and claimed asylum on the grounds that they had been part of the Yellow Bird Organization and had assisted many dissidents to escape to Hong Kong. Aside from the confirmation of their roles from the Yellow Bird organizers, it was relatively easy to check their story from the information already accumulated.

Their presence in Hong Kong was a major embarrassment and it was very difficult to arrange onward passage. The United States had no interest in low ranking servicemen, in contrast to the artillery colonel who had come through a few weeks earlier but eventually passage was arranged. To a large extent the flow of dissidents now dried up with only the occasional land border crosser. At this time the Immigration Service decided that it now had the capability to assume full responsibility for asylum seekers so the Cowboy and his officers were able to return to their normal routine duties.

In recognition of their efforts, all the officers in the teams received Commissioner's or Commanding Officer's Commendations which were celebrated in the time honoured police tradition of a 'Baai San' before the Kwan Dei, followed by a meal in a good restaurant and, for those who were still able, a night on the town.

Chapter Twenty

HONG KONG AND THE FUTURE

His Excellency The Governor of Hong Kong is the symbolic representative of Her Majesty The Queen and his authority for this role rests with the Letters Patent and the Royal Instructions. These documents authorize the establishment of an executive council or cabinet to assist His Excellency in reaching major policy decisions. The Executive Council comprises five *ex officio* members and nine appointed members, the latter usually drawn from the senior members of the Legislative Council and their nomination by the Governor had to be endorsed by the Secretary of State for Foreign and Commonwealth Affairs.

The Legislative Council is responsible for the routine administration of Hong Kong and originally comprised *ex officio*, official and unofficial members. The *ex officio* members are the same as the *ex officio* Members of the Executive Council with the exception of the Commander British Forces who withdrew from the council in 1966. The official members were heads of various important government departments and the unofficial members were nominated by the Governor from within the community. These unofficial members were drawn from various professions and usually included bankers, financiers, lawyers, trade union leaders, educationists and industrialists. The role of the unofficial members was not to act as the 'opposition' but rather to provide Government with the benefit of the expertise they had in their professional field.

The government officials met regularly in the course of their duties and the unofficial members also held regular meetings.

Much of the work of the members was carried out in committee or by way of circulation of consultation papers with a result that by the time a motion formally came before the Council it already reflected the consensus of the members and the actual public meeting was merely a 'rubber stamp' exercise. In a way this reflected the nature of oriental culture in that there would be no public 'loss of face' or embarrassment if a member's view was not upheld by the majority of the other members.

To Westerners brought up on a diet of confrontational politics with opposition parties almost automatically opposing whatever the Government proposed as a point of principle, the conduct of the Legislative Council left a lot to be desired. In defence of the Westerners it must be admitted that Hong Kong government rule was not the result of open and heated debate, nor were the Members of the Council acting on public mandate as the result of free and open elections. Issues were not clouded by any party policy and the law makers were not professional, career politicians but successful persons in their own spheres who provided honest and unbiased input to the production of effective government. The system worked successfully in that decisions were made in the best interests of the colony as whole, rather than in the interests of party politics even if sometimes the decisions might be unpopular with the general public. Certainly, Hong Kong was one of the few places in the world which did not have a budget deficit each year but was a highly successful economic entity.

However, in the eighties the pressure for a more open and democratic government which was accountable publicly to the people increased and a limited form of franchise was introduced. This took the form of functional constituencies in which various professions became constituencies and members of a profession would elect a member rather than the Governor select the member.

It was against this background that the Sino-British

Agreement on the future of Hong Kong was signed in 1984 and much was made of the expression 'One Country Two Systems', which was understood to mean that Hong Kong would continue to be governed in a similar manner to the existing system whilst China followed the Communist road. In response to voiced feelings of doubt and uncertainty expressed in Hong Kong, DENG Xiaoping gave a public undertaking that there would be no change for fifty years after China assumed sovereignty over Hong Kong.

Unlike statements of many Western politicians any public commitment by a senior Chinese leader, such as this by DENG, is totally valid. However, there is a problem in that the commitment is for no change in the style of administration that existed in 1984, but the British have introduced sweeping changes in the interim often without any prior consultation with Beijing. Naturally, Beijing view these changes with suspicion and believe that they are part of a subversive plot by the 'perfidious Albia' to retain power or influence over Hong Kong post 1997.

Over the last decade the Joint Liaison Committee has been in almost continual meetings in an attempt to interpret the finer points of the implementation of the Joint Declaration. Almost simultaneously there has been a growth in demand for greater democracy in Hong Kong, motivated to a great extent by a desire to ensure that the present freedoms and liberties are retained after 1997. The affair in Tiananmen Square in June 1989 really focused the sense of unease that lurked in the minds of most Hong Kong residents, whilst the massive public support in Hong Kong for the students raised the suspicions of the leadership in Beijing.

The public utterances of many of the leaders of the Hong Kong Alliance in support of the Patriotic Democratic Movement in China, which included calls for the overthrow, by violence if necessary, of the authoritarian government in Beijing and the organization of finance and escape routes such

221

as the Yellow Bird Operation did little to comfort the leaders in Beijing when many of the leaders, such as Martin Lee, SZETO-Wah, and CHEUNG Man-Kwong, had not recanted their previous public utterances and were now the advocates of greater democracy in Hong Kong.

It was in this atmosphere of increasing distrust by the Beijing government and public unease in Hong Kong that Chris Patten became the first politician to be appointed to the post of Governor of Hong Kong. Patten is an extremely astute and very personable politician who came from the Left Wing of the Conservative Party. As far as Beijing was concerned he was just a minor player, a failed politician in that, although the Conservative Party had won the General Election, he had not been re-elected in his Bath constituency, had lost the post of Chairman of the Conservative Party and had no pretensions to any particular knowledge or insight of Asia in general or Hong Kong in particular.

He upset the Hong Kong Establishment by turning up for the ceremonial arrival of His Excellency the Governor in an ill-fitting lounge suit, which did not meet around his midriff, and his shirt tail hanging out, rather than the traditional formal dress uniform of his post. His disregard of formality may have expressed his attitude as a 'man of the people' but was interpreted by many as a slight on the royal family whom he represented, and an indication of his indifference to the tradition and spirit of Hong Kong. He went on to compound this impression by publicly confronting the Beijing leaders in his first policy address to the Legislative Council by declaring future objectives and policies which had not been negotiated within the Joint Liaison Committee and challenged the Beijing government to come to terms with him. To many, these moves by Patten were an indication of an open and aggressive stance towards negotiations with Beijing. To more realistic minds it was a case of 'too little too late'.

It is not surprising that Patten has yet to be invited to Beijing for discussions whilst his three immediate predecessors regularly visited Beijing and Sir Edward Youde actually died in Beijing during a routine visit. The more cynical observers in Hong Kong suspect that Patten is merely using his time in Hong Kong as a platform from which to challenge for the leadership of the Conservative Party, hence his many high profile visits to world leaders, particularly Bill Clinton.

There is still more than a year to go before China resumes sovereignty over Hong Kong and much can change in that time. If the 'Old Guard' remain in positions of influence in Beijing then there is the danger that their sense of naturalistic patriotism will overcome the pragmatism of the 'Young Guard' to the detriment of the economic stability of Hong Kong as everything that symbolizes British Rule is dismantled. If the 'Young Guard' prevail then a more pragmatic policy is likely to be followed and Hong Kong will be used as a precedent for the future resumption of sovereignty over Taiwan.

Although the British government have many times in the past pontificated about the moral obligations to Hong Kong and its inhabitants, it is more concerned with pressing issues at home particularly the European Community and the future of Hong Kong is of little political importance.

The only people who are likely to suffer are the inhabitants of Hong Kong, many of whom were born and raised under the protection of the British Crown but are now to be abandoned. One Hong Kong Chinese expressed it in the following terms, 'We are but the children of a junior concubine and now the family is casting us out without any clothes.'

EPILOGUE

The Cowboy became aware of someone's presence intruding upon his reverie and opened his eyes with a tired effort. A wide smile came into focus and he realized that one of the cabin staff was trying to attract his attention. The smile was distorting as she informed him that the aircraft would be landing at Heathrow in less than an hour and it was time for breakfast. He declined the offer and requested orange juice. He raised the window blind and blinked at the sunlight which beamed into the cabin. Looking out of the porthole, he caught a glimpse of the sea and white cliffs which he presumed to be Dover. It still gave him a kick to be flying through the same airspace in which the Battle of Britain had been fought over fifty years before. He had been raised on stories of the 'Gallant Few' and even now, in his mind's eye, he could see the Spitfires and Hurricanes thrusting into the skies and almost hear the snarl of the Merlin engines.

Although he was now approaching Heathrow Airport he was still mentally 10,000 miles away in Hong Kong. He was one of the lucky people who were able to leave Hong Kong before 1997. Over the last thirty-odd years he had learnt to respect the integrity and energy of the Chinese people, particularly those who made Hong Kong the vibrant, prosperous citadel into which it had developed during that time. He had also learnt to distrust the old ogres who ruled the People's Republic of China from the shadows.

Opinions varied as to the future prospects for Hong Kong but he could not avoid a vague but deep feeling of unease

224

about the future and a sense of shame that British politicians had once again travelled the road to political expediency and not followed the path of honourable men. Trade links with China had been considered more important than any moral obligations to the inhabitants of Hong Kong. The majority of the population had either risked their lives to flee from Communist Party oppression or were the children of parents who had fled China and had been born in Hong Kong under the protection of the British Crown. Now the blanket of security was to be torn away and they were offered less than those who had lived in former colonies that had achieved independence.

Although many of the residents of Hong Kong were refugees from China the majority still retained some degree of pride in their Motherland. An understandable form of patriotism or national pride since an American Democrat does not love America the less if there is a Republican government nor does a British Socialist love Britain the less if there is a Conservative government. Some of the people had always harboured a resentment of British Colonial Rule and looked forward to China resuming sovereignty over Hong Kong and others took a more practical or pragmatic approach and just hoped that the change in rule would not affect their lives. Some would welcome the departure of the British on the assumption that they would become the new fat cats and live in splendour on Victoria Peak but he feared that these hopes would be dashed as the British colonialists would only be replaced by Mainland cadres who had the correct 'guangxi' (connections). There would probably be a major confrontation between the Hong Kong Communists and their Mainland colleagues as they fought over the spoils of the 'new' Hong Kong.

He wondered vaguely just why he was returning to Wales when he could just as easily have emigrated to Australia or the United States and realized that it was just a comfortable form of national pride to return to the place of his birth. He was now just a 55-year-old widower who had reached his sell-by date far earlier than he had anticipated and, he reflected bitterly, had achieved little in a life time in Hong Kong.

Not that he had been particularly ambitious or career oriented and had been content to reach the rank of Senior Superintendent with virtually his own independent command for the last twelve years in the rural New Territories, allowing him to indulge his instincts for street work rather than become yet another desk-bound administrator in Headquarters. He had seen too many officers lurch from crisis to crisis following promotion beyond their actual capability. There is a Chinese phrase 'Ling wai kaai haau mok wai ngau hau' which loosely translates as 'It is better to be the beak of a chicken than the rump of an ox'. In reality he had been one of the small cogs that had maintained Colonial Rule over Hong Kong in the arrogant assumption that to be born British gave one the inherent right to rule the world.

Now all was changing and somehow he was feeling as lost as any other refugee would be, approaching the British Isles.

Had it all been worth the effort?